AGEING WITH DISABILITY

A lifecourse perspective

Edited by
Eva Jeppsson Grassman and Anna Whitaker

First published in Great Britain in 2013 by

Policy Press
University of Bristol
Fourth Floor
Beacon House
Queen's Road
Bristol BS8 1QU
UK
t: +44 (0)117 331 4054
f: +44 (0)117 331 4093
tpp-info@bristol.ac.uk
www.policypress.co.uk

North America office:
Policy Press
c/o The University of Chicago Press
1427 East 60th Street
Chicago, IL 60637, USA
t: +1 773 702 7700
f: +1 773-702-9756
sales@press.uchicago.edu
www.press.uchicago.edu

British Library Cataloguing in Publication Data
A catalogue record for this book is available from the British Library.

Library of Congress Cataloging-in-Publication Data
A catalog record for this book has been requested.

ISBN 978 1 44730 522 4 hardcover

Cover design: Policy Press
Front cover: image kindly supplied by istock

Contents

Notes on contributors

Per Bülow is a clinical lecturer in health and society at the Psychiatric Department of Ryhov County Hospital in Jönköping, Sweden. His research focuses on questions concerning mental disability and ageing and on recovery from schizophrenia and other psychotic disorders. He has also published works on the deinstitutionalisation of psychiatric care in Sweden.

Lotta Holme is a senior lecturer in education, with focus on special education, at the Department of Behavioural Sciences and Learning at Linköping University, Sweden. She is also linked to the National Institute for the Study of Ageing and Later Life (NISAL) and participates in the research programme Disability, Life Course and Ageing. Holme teaches special education at the teacher training programme at Linköping University. Her research interests include disability, history, ageing; disability and identity, as well as questions concerning students with disabilities in higher education.

Eva Jeppsson Grassman, who until recently held a chair as professor at the National Institute for the Study of Ageing and Later Life (NISAL) at Linköping University, is now active as professor emeritus. The focus of her research is on welfare, disability, ageing and civil society. Her publications include work on the lifecourse and disability, end-of-life issues, voluntary organisations and ageing, informal caregiving and the role of the Church of Sweden from a welfare perspective. She is the director of the research programmes Disability, Life Course and Ageing, and Forms of Care in Later Life: Agency, Place, Time and Life Course.

Tommy Svensson is professor of sociology at the Department of Behavioural Sciences and Learning, Division of Pedagogy and Sociology, at Linköping University. His major research interest is in the area of sociology of mental illness, but in recent years, he has also studied problems related to long-term sick leave and the social psychological aspects of occupational rehabilitation in preparation for returning to work.

Annika Taghizadeh Larsson is a senior lecturer at the National Institute for the Study of Ageing and Later Life (NISAL) at Linköping University. Her research interests mainly comprise questions and issues at the intersection of social gerontology and disability studies, including social policy and welfare for older people and people with disabilities, ageing with early onset impairments. She is presently studying dementia and citizenship.

Cristina Joy Torgé is a PhD candidate at the National Institute for the Study of Ageing and Later Life (NISAL) at Linköping University. Her academic background is in philosophy, medical and public health ethics and health. Her chapter in this book is based on her dissertation work in the field of ageing and later life, with focus on disability and mutual care.

Anna Whitaker is a senior lecturer and associate professor of social work at the Department of Social Sciences, Ersta Sköndal University College. She is also affiliated with the National Institute for the Study of Ageing and Later Life (NISAL) at Linköping University. Her research includes issues on death and dying, end-of-life in old age, the ageing and dying body, family care in institution-based elder care, ageing with disability and the role of family carers. Another area of interest concerns the Church of Sweden and its role in end-of-life care and bereavement. In her current research she is studying the disbandment process, and the changing meaning of personal possessions in later life transitions.

Acknowledgements

The work on which this book is based was funded mainly by research grants from the Swedish Research Council (Dnr 2005-1056) and the Swedish Council for Working Life and Social Research (Dnr 2006-1621). We are thankful for their support.

Foreword

Judith Phillips

Ageing with disability: A lifecourse perspective offers a well-informed, critical approach to the debates in the fields of disability and ageing. As the title suggests it views disability through the lens of the lifecourse, addressing the impact of multiple disabilities over time and on the different phases of life. The book challenges our stereotypes of 'successful ageing', particularly in the context of the social model of disability. New questions are raised and discussed, such as 'What does it mean to age with a physical or mental disability, and what care resources are available?' 'How do older people make sense of disability, and what is the meaning of care in such contexts?' The chapter authors offer an excellent mix of theory and evidence, within comparative policy contexts, to explore these questions.

Students, academics, professionals and policy makers will be attracted to this text which addresses the social model of disability, and to the series 'Ageing and the Lifecourse' on the latest research, theory, policy and practice developments in ageing.

ONE

Ageing with disability: An introduction

Eva Jeppsson Grassman and Anna Whitaker

Background

The risk of acquiring impairments of various kinds increases as we grow older. Such old age-related impairments are not the ones at issue in this book, however. Instead, the focus is on people who have acquired impairments or chronic illness earlier in life, perhaps during childhood, adolescence or young adulthood, and who have had better chances than those in previous generations to live long lives. The aim of the book is to discuss – from a lifecourse perspective – what it means to live a long life, to age and to become old for people who have disabilities acquired early in life. The key questions are:

- What does it mean to live a long life and to age with a physical or mental disability?
- How have the lives of disabled people been affected by an era marked by disability reforms and identity politics?
- What does it mean to be an ageing parent and continue to care for an adult disabled child?
- How are we to understand 'couplehood' in the case when both parties are disabled?

These are questions that have been studied only to a limited extent in disability research as well as in ageing research to date, but are explored in the following chapters.

In general, we know relatively little about disabled people's lives over time and the meaning of living with a disability for many years, to grow old and to be old. One explanation for this may be that the possibility of a long life and of growing old with disabilities is a relatively recent phenomenon. It is only since the Second World War that we have had identifiable generations of disabled people who have lived through different ages and reached an advanced age (Strauss and Shavelle, 1998; Mattsson and Glad, 2005; Nilsson et al, 2005), and when/where the lifecourse concept may appear to be relevant. Zarb (1993), who studied the living conditions of people who lived a long time with disabilities, noted that even if there are similarities between this group and other non-disabled groups of the same age, the group also has its own particular experiences shaped by life with disability. Jeppsson Grassman has come to the same conclusions (2008). Yet there is a conspicuous lack of knowledge concerning the long lives and ageing of disabled people and the challenges they face, as pointed out by several scholars in recent years. This book is one of few to address these issues. Research on disability and ageing has, to date, generally been focused on disability issues in older people rather than what it is like to live for many years and to grow older with lifelong disabilities (Putnam, 2002; Verbrugge and Yang 2003; Avlund, 2004). Similarly, little research has been conducted focusing on what it means to spend many years as a parent, sibling or spouse to a disabled person in need of help and care (DeMarle and le Roux, 2001; Jeppsson Grassman et al, 2009). Yet a disability that affects the individual contributes greatly to the shaping of the lifecourse of all members of a family. In the Western world in general there is now a new and growing demand for better knowledge about these different groups, not least in policy planning.

Illness, disability and survival

A life with disability involves particular experiences. How common is this experience in Western countries? This is a question that is not easy to answer unequivocally as 'disability' is not a clearly defined concept. The social definition of disability, which implies that barriers in the environment create disability, makes it difficult to decide how we define 'disabled' people as a group, or whether we even should (Swedish Government Official Report, 2001:56). At the same time, in many situations, there is a need for definitions of individual disabilities, for instance in order for the individual to acquire rightful entitlements. Barron et al (2000) discuss two different types of definitions. One is based on administrative criteria (and identifies the various groups affected by certain social reforms and entitlements). With this definition the population of disabled people tends to become rather narrow. The second definition is based on individual criteria by focusing on self-reported physical or mental limitations in functions. This type of definition may be criticised for being based too much on the individual experience of illness and loss. On the other hand, an environmentally, or socially, defined concept is often fluid and difficult to manage. In light of this reasoning, one can easily understand that the question of how many people are disabled does not have a precise answer. With a reasonably broad definition, based on self-reported impairments in various groups, it has been estimated that, in the year 2000, around 13 per cent of the Swedish population aged 16-64 had a disability. In the age group 65–84, the equivalent percentage was approximately 45 per cent (Swedish Government Official Report, 2001:56; See also Statistics Sweden, 2009). The pattern is similar in other European countries. A survey conducted within the European Union (EU) found that around 15 per cent of the total populations of the member states aged 16-64 reported some form of long-standing health disorder or disability (Eurostat, 2003). This means that disability concerns large populations. However, this definition says nothing about the severity of the disability, of its consequences, about how long people have had their disabilities, or about age at onset of the disability.

Disabled people are not a homogeneous group. Heterogeneity is illustrated by the fact that disability is caused by a large number of different illnesses and injuries, which may also have various consequences within the same diagnostic group. Disabled people are of different ages, with onset of disability at various times, and they have had their disabilities for various lengths of time. Disabilities vary with time, age and gender. The implications of various disabilities can be highly variable depending on the mentioned conditions. We must, for example, assume that there are important differences between the experience of an older pensioner who acquires a moderate disability late in life, and that of a person who has been disabled since childhood as a result of a severe and chronic illness. These various conditions have a bearing on the main question of this book. The groups on whose experiences the chapters of this book are based have in common that their lives have been shaped by severe disabilities, in most cases due to serious, chronic illnesses – physical or mental. Examples include diabetes, multiple sclerosis, spina bifida, schizophrenia and various other chronic illnesses.

Longer life but with high morbidity

There is no indication that the incidence of injuries and illnesses that can cause disability is decreasing in society, generally speaking. The overall picture is multifaceted and varies with type of disability. The risk of developing certain illnesses that can cause disabilities, such as cardiovascular disease, decreased during the period 1987–2002. However, increasing numbers of people are being diagnosed with diabetes, and mental illness has increased among young people in Europe (National Board of Health and Welfare, 2005; WHO, 2009). The risk of acquiring disabilities increases with age. On the other hand, just as life expectancy has increased (and is increasing) for Western populations as a whole, it has also increased for people with various illnesses and disabilities. It is difficult to find quantitative data on the survival patterns of different groups of ill and of disabled people. However, there is research that indicates increased chances of survival, notably for people with some of the disabilities addressed in this book. Yet this does not necessarily mean that they have the same longevity as populations in general. For instance, severe mental illness is associated with a shorter life in many Western countries, notably in the Nordic countries (Wahlbeck et al, 2011). The 'extended life' with illness and disability does not in any simple way imply a life with less morbidity and suffering, or even the same degree of problems or suffering over time.

Advances in medical technology, better diagnostics and therapies, as well as welfare systems generally, have contributed to these patterns of development. One example is spina bifida, a condition that causes substantial disability for the individual. Prior to the 1950s, few survived, but with the new methods introduced in the 1950s, more and more people with this condition survive, and today they are regarded as 'the new survivors' (Wong and Paulozzi, 2001). Their degree of longevity has increased steadily over recent decades, while, at the same time, their level of disability means that they live at high risk of cumulative impairments and with a mortality that is much higher than in the general population (Mattsson and Gladh, 2005). Cerebral palsy is another example. Increased survival has been observed over time, and today many individuals with cerebral palsy can foresee a life expectancy that is equal to the population average (Evans et al, 1990; Strauss and Shavelle, 1998; Himmelman, 2006).

Diabetes and polio are further examples. Type-1 (juvenile) diabetes, which mainly affects children and adolescents, is a severe, chronic disease, but the survival pattern changed dramatically when insulin therapy was introduced in the 1920s (Feudtner, 2003). Improved therapies subsequently increased long-term survival. Among those who acquired the illness in the 1940s in Sweden, about one third has now survived for at least 50 years with the illness (Nilsson et al, 2005). Polio has been eradicated in Western countries thanks to universal vaccination, but for those who acquired this illness earlier, mainly prior to 1960, and survived, the illness has been shown to cause serious complications after many years, so-called post-polio (Myrvang, 2006).

It is necessary to emphasise that the various examples given here are used as illustrations of the starting point and thesis of this book; it is now possible to live many years and to age with severe chronic illnesses and disabilities. It is not an *uncommon* experience, but at the same time, the long life is associated with *particular* experiences.

Ageing and the lifecourse approach

The book is based on a lifecourse perspective, which means that we assume that life today and the meaning of disability is best understood in the context of the *dynamics of the whole lifecourse* and with an approach in which *ageing is seen as a lifelong process*. With this view, central concerns are *when* an individual became disabled, *for how long* she or he has had a disability, *how* it has affected the different stages of life and *how old* the individual is at the time of reminiscing on his or her life with disability. In this approach, temporality takes on multidimensional meanings. This is not least because the *historical time* in which individuals live also has a central significance for this perspective. The individual's place in history, in the spatial and temporal sense, operates in the shaping of that individual's life (Giele and Elder, 1998; Elder et al, 2003; Bornat, 2004). Additionally, a lifecourse approach contributes to illuminating the considerable variation in people's experiences of their time, due to differences in individual resources and positions. Yet there is also a dimension of *shared experience* that has to do with conditions such as age, sex, social class or geographical connectedness (Alwin, 1995; Giele and Elder, 1998). Following this reasoning it can be assumed that disabled people share specific experiences, yet also have different experiences, depending on, for instance, the historical context in which the individual lives. *Family and generational relations* are also significant and contribute greatly in forming an individual's lifecourse (Hareven, 2000, 2001; Mills, 2000).

Furthermore, the lifecourse can be described as age-graded patterns of development embedded in social institutions in a specific historical era (Elder et al, 2003). Irrespective of point of departure, the lifecourse may be regarded as having its personal, individual shape, but is also influenced by institutionalised norms regarding life's phases – a kind of established social timetable that is more or less universal or characteristic of the historical point in time (Närvänen, 2004). The concept of normality plays the role of compass here. In discussing the concept of the lifecourse, the 'typical', 'normal' lifecourse is all too often the starting point. It has been pointed out that we need to study atypical or deviant lifecourses in order to broaden our knowledge about life and ageing (Ansello and Eustis, 1992; Zarb, 1993; Leisering, 2003; Jeppsson Grassman, 2008). Thus, based on a number of qualitative studies, the book's central approach involves the question of how the lifecourse, life transitions and life today are shaped for disabled people and their families who have lived under certain historical conditions.

A lifecourse perspective to old age also implies that later life must be interpreted within the context of the individual's whole biography. Usually, studies of the lifecourse tend to operate separately from gerontological studies (Grenier, 2012). The reverse situation, the absence of lifecourse approaches in gerontological studies, is equally true. In this book, with its lifecourse approach, the chapters particularly aim at shedding light on the conditions and meaning of old age within the framework of the unique experience of a long life with disability. In this way, the book contributes with new insights, and adds new knowledge both to gerontology *and* to disability studies. Neither discipline has, to date, paid much attention to these particular issues. This also goes for themes such as the impact of disability on the shaping of particular life transitions, and on the meaning of age norms. Other themes addressed have to do with end of life and time left. Furthermore, the findings concerning life with disability in old age challenge, in various ways, dominant ideas and conceptualisations about successful ageing and the third age – not only as addressed in current gerontological debates; They also challenge dominant norms about what a life with disability 'ought to be' in order to embody modern disability ideals in old age.

Studying the imprints of history on biography

To what extent is it possible to capture the interplay between biographical and historical time? What can we really say about history's impact on individuals' lives? This is a difficult methodological undertaking and entails considering a number of issues that have been widely acknowledged and discussed in (lifecourse) research (see Bertaux, 1981; Mortimer and Shanahan, 2003; Bornat, 2004; Grenier, 2012). Different types of methodological designs and biographical approaches have been used in the studies presented in the chapters. One study has a unique *prospective* design in which a small group of disabled individuals were followed up over a period of 30 years and interviewed on six occasions (see Chapter Two). The other chapters in the book build on extensive *retrospective* interviews carried out at one time, but with somewhat different approaches, emphasising different aspects of the lived life. For example, in Chapter Three, a political lifecourse perspective is used to shed light on the biographical stories about disability, political activism and identity and in what way this shapes the experiences of ageing and old age. In Chapter Five, different life story approaches are combined to capture the experiences and the stories about living a long life with mental disabilities. Another biographical approach is used in Chapter Seven, in which disabled couples are interviewed together (dyadic interviews) to explore the (mutual) meaning of care, disability, reciprocity and ageing.

Besides researching the past and present in people's life stories, a lifecourse perspective and a biographical approach also implies an interest in the *future*. To date, curiously enough, this dimension has seldom been addressed in lifecourse research. In the various chapters in the book, issues concerning the future are highlighted, revealing hopes, fears and concerns about the future among the participants. *Time left* turns out to be a central concept (see also Jeppsson Grassman, 2012). What becomes apparent in the chapters is not only that past experiences shape the future, but that the future also contributes to shaping the past and present. What the various methodological strategies also have in common is that they have provided analytic tools that have increased the possibility of identifying *if* and *in what way* the historical era – with various reforms and social changes – appears to have had an impact on the participants' personal experiences and lives with disability. This question is emphasised to various extents in the different chapters.

The historical era

What are the historical conditions that form the time frame for the studies referred to in this book (which is the era from 1960 up to the present)? The general trends of development during this time have been similar in many ways in the European countries, and increasingly influenced by global processes. Yet it is important to underline that the specific societal context that is the point of departure here is Sweden and its political, economic and cultural conditions (Ahrne et al, 2003).

The time frame encompasses first the years of 1960–75, characterised by economic growth and by optimism concerning the future. These were some of the 'golden years of the welfare state' in many countries, when important programmes in the welfare arena were implemented. Higher education was made accessible for broader segments of the Swedish population, and women started to enter the labour market on a large scale. After a period of structural recession in the late 1970s, the later 1980s represented a new phase of economic growth. Full employment was a major political goal that was (almost) achieved. Even disabled people were to gain access to the labour market, and new policies and legislation protected their jobs. In a general sense, the 1970s and the 1980s came to represent a switch of paradigm: the earlier rather one-sided emphasis on the duty of the individual to adapt was replaced by a more environmentally oriented approach in various areas, such as at work and in schools. It was primarily the environment that was to be adapted to the needs of the individual, not the reverse. There was a great belief in 'the normal' and its beneficial impact in various types of situations. There is a parallel here to the disability policies that were to be developed. The staying-in-place ideology gained ground in elder care and would eventually also do so in psychiatric care. This was mirrored in the de-institutionalisation processes that were annexed to the idea of normalisation.

This time of economic expansion was succeeded by the years 1991–2000, which was a period of recession that brought a financial crisis and increasing unemployment in Sweden. The implementation of far-reaching public cutbacks was the main strategy to deal with the crisis. As in several other European countries this was the time when deregulation of the welfare state was initiated and privatisation was gradually implemented in several areas. A market paradigm came to dominate the public discourse as well as policies. During this time a very important, and costly, reform in disability policy was passed – the implementation of the 1993 Act concerning Support and Service for Persons with Certain Functional Impairments – which enabled increased autonomy and choice for severely disabled people.[1]

The socioeconomic and cultural gaps increased during the 1990s in Sweden, and have continued to do so. This has turned out to be a common pattern in many other Western countries as well. In spite of economic recovery in the 2000s, these gaps in society have tended to continue to increase. 'Flexibility' and 'choice' have become guiding principles. Sweden was one of the European countries that managed to get through the economic crisis of 2008 reasonably successfully. Yet the higher level of unemployment persists – it is three times as high as in the 1960s. It is important to note that the era that has been given a sketchy description here also contains the expansion of civil society, where many voluntary organisations were created as a result of endeavours by patient groups, disabled people and families fighting for common social causes.

Development of disability policies in Europe

Disabled people who have lived through the late 1900s and the early 2000s have been the subject of – and sometimes have themselves been active in – the creation of a range of disability reforms that may have shaped their lifecourse. The development of disability policies in Europe can, from a lifecourse perspective, be structured into several phases, based on central, time-bound concepts and ideas. These concepts have been (and still are) based on strong ideological and political values. The development can be viewed as a movement from one paradigmatic model regarding disability to another, from a medical model towards a social model that has finally turned into a somewhat more eclectic formulation of what disability implies. These models have orchestrated a development of modern disability policies in gradual phases. Disability policy covers a wide range of quite different fields. The overall aim is to enable disabled people to have the same living conditions as most other citizens in society. Reforms aimed at increasing accessibility in society are important parts of disability policy. They apply to areas such as assistive technology, transport, housing, education and employment.

Before 1950, the traditional view of disabled people as crippled, deaf and dumb, and so on, which had dominated since the 19th century, was hardly contested in Western countries. Disabled people were categorised and separated from society through placement in institutions, special schools and by other particular measures. The first modern ideas regarding disability policies were introduced in the late 1950s and in the 1960s. A driving force in this change was the new principle of *normalisation* (Nirje, 1980). The Nordic countries, not least Sweden, played a pioneering role here (Gustavsson et al, 2005; Shakespeare, 2006). The overarching idea behind this principle was the integration of disabled people into society. This principle, which framed the first phase of modern disability policies, also represented a first step towards challenging the medical model of interpretation in which problems and shortcomings, such as illness and impairments, are assigned to the individual, who must compensate for them. During the period 1950-60 the disability rights movement gradually became more influential in Western societies. The struggle for equal rights and equal opportunities was inspired by other social rights movements.

In the 1980s, disability policies went through a radical phase of development when the concept that disability was relative to the environment was introduced in many countries (WHO, 2001). The guiding principle was that 'the handicap' was created through shortcomings in the environment – the physical, social, political and so on. In Anglo Saxon countries the social model of disability was formulated as an alternative approach to a medical view of disability. The social model emphasises that disability is constructed by discrimination and society's inaccessibility. Thus, the problem no longer resides only with the individual, but also exists in relation to external demands for functions and abilities. In the Nordic countries, the social model corresponds closest to the so-called 'Nordic relational model of disability' (Shakespeare, 2006) that was developed in the 1980s. It sees disability as 'environmentally relative' and posits that disability arises as a consequence of a mismatch in the relationship between the individual and the environment. It has been very influential, not least rhetorically, in the Nordic countries, and has permeated policies and practical measures that have been implemented in the past three decades.

Since the 1990s, there has been a movement towards more eclectic and holistic approaches to disability and 'what it is', involving both the individual and the environment, and the interaction between them. The standard rules of the World Health Organization (WHO), issued in 2001, build on this general view (WHO, 2001). We need the social model *as well as* the medical model if we are to fully understand the conditions of people with illness and impairments in society (see, for example, Priestley, 2003). Shakespeare (2006) argues that such a holistic view of disability is necessary to escape the dead-end street that, according to him, the social model has imposed on disability studies. Key concepts in disability policies today are *citizenship*, *equality* and *full participation*. In Sweden, the implementation of the 1993 Act concerning Support and Service for Persons with Certain Functional Impairments, together with the 1993 Assistance Compensation Act, represented significant steps towards 'full citizenship' for disabled people in the sense that they would have the opportunity to take control over their own living conditions. The implementation of these Acts has turned out to have a great impact, both ideologically and factually. To our knowledge, equivalent Acts do not exist in other European countries, yet there is legislation that has the same purpose. One example is Norway. In the UK, furthermore, local authority social services departments have, since 1997, been able to provide disabled people with so-called direct payments with which to employ their own personal assistants (Glendinning et al, 2000). At present, direct payments may be available to those who are 'disabled and aged 16 or over', 'a parent or carer aged 16 or over (including people with parental responsibility for a disabled child)' or 'an older person'. However, according to official statistics, direct payments are, as in the Swedish case, still a minority form of provision (Riddell, 2008).

In the area of mental disability the development has been both similar and in some ways different from the described process. More than for other groups of disabled people, the history of mental illness is linked to great institutions, so-called asylums, and to inhuman treatment. Up until 40–50 years ago, being mentally ill meant being admitted to a psychiatric hospital, often for a long period. An important change started to take place in the 1960s and 1970s, when the majority of the industrialised countries initiated a de-institutionalisation of psychiatric care and reorganised it into community-based care. The timing, tempo and financing of this process differed, however, from country to country. Political systems, according to Goodwin (1997), were crucial for how the process developed. Countries with social democratic governments, like the Nordic countries, started the process later than other regime types and proceeded slowly, focusing on social rights and fairness (Goodwin, 1997). The fact that people were discharged from psychiatric hospitals and into the community actualised the concept of 'disability' for people with mental disorders. In Sweden, where the de-institutionalisation process started late, the concept of mental disability (instead of mental illness) was also introduced late. It was only in 1995, following the introduction of the psychiatric care reform aimed at improving the lives of the mentally disabled in the community, that the concept was implemented and written into the legislation. Yet at least in Sweden, the impact today of principles such as citizenship, equality and full participation seems much less noticeable in policy and debate regarding people with mental disabilities than it does regarding people with physical or intellectual disabilities.

Looking back on 50 years of modern disability policies and changes, a conclusion to be drawn must be that the prerequisites for better living conditions and opportunities for disabled people have improved – in Sweden, and in many other European countries. Yet there is more to be achieved. Furthermore, other societal processes, such as those described in the previous section, also have an important effect on how life actually turns out for disabled people growing old in our time.

Outline of the book

From various lifecourse perspectives, and with the described time as context, the authors in this book explore what it means to live a long life and to grow old with disabilities. Contrasting images of disability, time, ageing, transitions and life after retirement and also patterns of common experiences are presented.

In Chapter Two, Eva Jeppsson Grassman focuses on the long life with disability, its characteristics and the impact of age and time on the shaping of the lifecourse. The discussion builds on results from a prospective study in which the author followed a group of chronically ill and visually impaired people, for 30 years, through repeated interviews. The framework of the chapter is employment, exit from the labour market and life after retirement. The author argues that these themes are shaped by the gradually failing and unpredictable body, which stands out as an over-arching, recurring theme in the interviews and which has to do with the long-term disabling consequences of chronic illness. The unpredictable body implies living with an uncertain future. This entails particular experiences that also influence the lived experience of old age. A conclusion drawn is that the bodily and temporal dimensions studied are complex: time with illness and disability, age, 'time left' and relational time – all these dimensions are interwoven in complex ways and according to changing patterns, in the studied lives, which are marked by illness complications and gradual functional loss.

Chapter Three, by Lotta Holme, explores how pioneers of the modern Swedish disability rights movement experience ageing. The main issue is how this special group of disabled people express their attitudes towards ageing and later life after a long life with disability, in the light of disability activism, politics and history. The chapter also examines perspectives and experiences of ageing in relation to what we usually call a 'normal' lifecourse. A 'political lifecourse perspective' is discussed in order to create an understanding of the links between experiences of disability, activism in the disability rights movement and a so-called 'normal' lifecourse. The chapter builds on interviews with eight disabled people in Sweden from 2008 to 2011. The informants have lived with disability for many years, they are devoted disability activists and have had leading positions in different areas in the modern Swedish disability rights movement. An implication of this is that the group in question has had more reason than most to learn about and profoundly reflect on disability issues, both in their personal lives and in connection with their positions in the movement.

In Chapter Four, Annika Taghizadeh Larsson deals with the opportunities and challenges of adopting a modern, leisurely active and self-fulfilling pensioner's lifestyle – to 'age successfully' – if you are a wheelchair user and relatively dependent on other people's support to manage daily tasks. The author illustrates how the general development in welfare, technical improvements and reforms, such as legislation on the adaptation of homes and personal assistance services, may actually enable some pensioners with extensive impairments to adopt a pensioner's lifestyle similar to the one called 'successful ageing'. This points to the importance of considering how social and environmental contexts may influence the meanings and consequences of 'becoming old' for disabled people. The author also discusses existing obstacles to such a lifestyle. Although the chapter highlights the many new facilities that may compensate for the consequences of disability in later life, the author discusses in her concluding remarks some possible advantages of a traditional, more 'passive' lifestyle ideal. This type of lifestyle may be beneficial for those who prefer a quiet life and for those who, for different reasons, do not meet the standards of a performance-oriented culture.

In Chapter Five, Per Bülow and Tommy Svensson discuss mental disability and ageing. The chapter is based on life story-oriented interviews with older people who have a very long personal experience of mental disability and psychiatric care. The chapter addresses the question of what it means to have lived a long life with severe mental disabilities and the social implications associated with this, in terms of experiences and perceptions of growing old. In the light of the participants' experiences and reflections on their lives, the authors discuss the extensive changes that have occurred during the last 50 years in society's way of organising care and treatment of mental illness.

In Chapter Six, Anna Whitaker focuses on ageing parents and their experience of providing care for a disabled child throughout the lifecourse, and discusses the ways in which this experience has shaped their lives. The point of departure is empirical findings that bring to light the complexity of these parents' experiences of their lifelong care responsibility. This responsibility remains during the adult life of the child – despite wide-ranging disability policy reforms, and despite extensive support and assistance through, for instance, personal assistants. The author reveals the parental experience of living close to a disabled child for a very long time and the impact of this on the parents' own personal lives. Furthermore, the chapter shows that thoughts about the future represent a fearful theme among the parents. What these life stories provide are biographies characterised by care and a care responsibility that extends even into the future.

In Chapter Seven, Cristina Joy Torgé discusses what it means to give and receive care when intimate partners choose to live and age together in spite of their long-term disabilities. The chapter is based on a qualitative study in which disabled couples aged 60 years and over were interviewed together. The author shows that care permeates the couples' lives, but that the long life of disability as well as a long time living together can obscure spousal care. Different care tasks – both physical and emotional help for the spouse – are parts of attempts to make everyday life work and maintain an equilibrium, but can also fulfil other purposes such as maintaining closeness and integrity as a couple. Care concerns are not limited to the present, they are also embodied and shared as two individuals think about how to maintain togetherness and a 'life like others', despite disabled embodiment and ageing. The author proposes the concept *we-work* not as a synonym for care but as an alternative concept that further shows how 'care' comes short in describing these couples' experiences.

The book is rounded off by Chapter Eight that consists of a summary and concluding remarks building on some salient themes that have been brought up in the preceding chapters.

Note

[1] In the late 1980s the first attempts to employ personal assistants were made in Sweden. In 1994 this Act, together with the 1993 Assistance Compensation Act, came into force. The latter was a rights law supplementing other legislation with the aim to 'promote equality in living conditions and full participation in the life of the community', for people with considerable and permanent functional impairments.

References

Ahrne, G., Roman, Ch. and Franzén, M. (2003) *Det sociala landskapet: En sociologisk beskrivning av Sverige från 1950-talet till början på 2000-tal* [*The social landscape: A sociological description of Sweden from the 1950s to the beginning of the 2000s*], Göteborg: Korpen.

Alwin, D.E. (1995) 'Taking time seriously: studying social change, social structure, and human lives', in P. Moen, G.H. Elder and K. Lüscher (eds) *Examining lives in context: Perspectives on the ecology of human development*, Washington, DC: American Psychological Association, pp 211-62.

Ansello, E.F. and Eustis, N.N. (eds) (1992) *Aging and disabilities: Seeking common ground*, New York: Baywood.

Avlund, K. (2004) *Disability in old age: Longitudinal population-based studies of the disablement process*, Copenhagen: Department of Social Medicine, Institute of Public Health, University of Copenhagen.

Barron, K., Michailakis, D. and Söder, M. (2000) 'Funktionshindrade och den offentliga hjälpapparaten' ['Disabled people and the public support system'], in M. Szebehely (ed) *Välfärd, vård och omsorg* [*Welfare and care*], Swedish Government Official Report, 2000:38, Stockholm: Fritzes, pp 137-70.

Bertaux, D. (ed) (1981) *Biography and society: The life history approach in the social sciences*, Beverly Hills, CA: Sage Publications.

Bornat, J. (2004) 'Oral history', in C. Seale, G. Giampietro, J. Gubrium and D. Silverman (eds) *Qualitative research practice*, London: Sage Publications, pp 34-47.

DeMarle, D. and le Roux, P. (2001) 'The life cycle and disability: experiences of discontinuity in child and family development', *Journal of Loss & Trauma*, vol 6, no 1, pp 29-43.

Elder, G.H. Jr, Kirkpatrick Johnson, M. and Crosnoe, R. (2003) 'The emergence and development of life course theory', in J.T. Mortimer and M.J. Shanahan (eds) *Handbook of the life course*, New York: Kluwer Academic, pp 3-19.

Eurostat (2003) *Statistics in focus. Populations and social conditions*, Theme 3-26/2003.

Evans, P.M., Evans, S.J. and Alberman, E. (1990) 'Cerebral palsy: why we must plan for survival', *Archives of Disease in Childhood*, vol 65, no 12, pp 1329-33.

Feudtner, C. (2003) *Bittersweet: Diabetes, insulin, and the transformation of illness*, Chapel Hill, NC: North Carolina Press.

Giele, J.Z. and Elder, G.H. (1998) 'Life course research: Development of a field', in J.Z. Giele and G.H. Elder (eds) *Methods of life course research: Qualitative and quantitative approaches*, Thousand Oaks, CA: Sage Publications, pp 5-27.

Glendinning, C., Halliwell, S., Jacobs, S., Rummery, K. and Tyrer, J. (2000) 'New kinds of care, new kinds of relationships: how purchasing services affects relationships in giving and receiving personal assistance', *Health and Social Care in the Community*, vol 8, no 3, pp 201-11.

Goodwin, S. (1997) *Comparative mental health policy: From institutional to community care*, London: Sage Publications.

Grenier, A. (2012) *Transition and the lifecourse: Challenging the constructions of 'growing old'*, Bristol: The Policy Press.

Gustavsson, A., Sandvin, J., Traustadóttir, R. and Tøssebro, J. (2005) *Resistance, reflection and change: Nordic disability research*, Lund: Studentlitteratur.

Hareven, T.K. (2000) *Families, history and social change: Lifecourse and cross-cultural perspectives*, Boulder, CO: Westview Press.

Hareven, T.K. (2001) 'The impact of family history and the life course on social history', in R. Wall, T.K Hareven and J. Ehmer (eds) *Family history revisited: Comparative perspectives*, Newark, DE: University of Delaware Press, pp 21-39.

Himmelman, K. (2006) *Cerebral palsy in Western Sweden: Epidemiology and function*, Gothenburg: Gothenburg University.

Jeppsson Grassman, E. (2012) 'Chronic illness, awareness of death and the ambiguity of peer identification', in D. Davies and C. Park (eds) *Emotion, identity and death: Mortality across disciplines*, Farnham: Ashgate, pp 15-28.

Jeppsson Grassman, E. (ed) (2008) *Att åldras med funktionshinder* [*Ageing with disability*], Lund: Studentlitteratur.

Jeppsson Grassman, E., Whitaker, A. and Taghizadeh Larsson, A. (2009) 'Family as failure. The role of informal helpgivers to disabled people in Sweden', *Scandinavian Journal of Disability Research*, vol 11, no 1, pp 35-49.

Leisering, L. (2003) 'Government and the life course', in J.T. Mortimer and M.J. Shanahan (eds) *Handbook of the life course*, New York: Kluwer Academic, pp 205-226.

Mattsson, S. and Gladh, G. (2005) 'Barn med ryggmärgsbråck blir vuxna!' ['Children with spina bifida are growing up!'], *Läkartidningen*, vol 102, no 37, pp 2566-70.

Mills, M. (2000) 'Providing space for time. The impact of temporality on life course research', *Time & Society*, vol 9, no 1, pp 91-127.

Mortimer, J.T. and Shanahan, M.J. (eds) *Handbook of the lifecourse*, New York: Kluwer Academic.

Myrvang, V.H. (2006) *Ut av arbeidslivet: Livsløp, mestring og identitet. En studie av personer med seinskader etter polio* [*Leaving working life: Lifecourse, coping and identity. A study of people with post-polio impairments*], NOVA report 1/06, Oslo: Oslo University.

National Board of Health and Welfare (2005) *Folkhälsorapport* [*Healthcare report*], Stockholm: Socialstyrelsen.

Nilsson, S.E., Nilsson, M.S., Nilsson, E.D. and Nilsson, P.M. (2005) 'Långtidsöverlevnaden vid diabetes har successivt förändrats' ['Gradually improved long-term survival in diabetes'], *Läkartidningen*, vol 102, no 28-29, pp 2066-70.

Nirje, B. (1980) 'The normalization principle', in R. Flynn and K.E. Nitsch (eds) *Normalization, social integration and community services*, Baltimore, MD: University Park Press, pp 31-49.

Närvänen, A.-L. (2004) 'Age, ageing and the life course', in B. Öberg, A.-L. Närvänen, E. Näsman and E. Olsson (eds) *Changing worlds and the ageing subject: Dimensions in the study of ageing and later life*, Aldershot: Ashgate, pp 65-80.

Priestley, M. (2003) *Disability: A life course approach*, Cambridge: Polity Press.

Putnam, M. (2002) 'Linking aging theory and disability models: increasing the potential to explore aging with physical impairment', *The Gerontologist*, vol 42, no 6, pp 799-806.

Riddell, S. (2008) 'Direct payments and disabled children and young people: the service of the future?', *Journal of Research in Special Educational Needs*, vol 8, pp 167-82.

Shakespeare, T. (2006) *Disability rights and wrongs*, London: Routledge.

Statistics Sweden (2009) *Funktionsnedsattas situation på arbetsmarknaden – 4:e kvartalet 2008* [*Labour market situation for disabled persons – 4th quarter 2008*], Stockholm: Statistics Sweden.

Strauss, D. and Shavelle, R. (1998) 'Life expectancy of adults with cerebral palsy', *Developmental Medicine & Child Neurology*, vol 40, no 6, pp 369-75.

Swedish Government Official Report (2001:56) *Funktionshinder och välfärd. Forskarantologi från Kommittén Välfärdsbokslut* [*Disability and welfare. A research anthology from the Welfare Commission*], Stockholm: Fritzes.

Verbrugge, L.M. and Yang, L. (2002) 'Ageing with disability and disability with ageing', *Journal of Disability Policy Studies*, vol 12, no 4, pp 253-67.

Wahlbeck, K., Westman, J., Nordentoft, M., Gissler, M. and Munk Larsen, T.. (2011) 'Outcomes of Nordic mental health systems: life expectancy of patients with mental disorders', *British Journal of Psychiatry*, vol 199, no 6, pp 453-8.

WHO (World Health Organization) (2001) *International classification of functioning, disability and health*, Geneva: WHO.

WHO (2009) *Global health risks. Mortality and burden of disease attributable to selected major risks*, Geneva: WHO.

Wong, L.-Y. and Paulozzi, L.J. (2001) 'Survival of infants with spina bifida: a population study, 1979-94', *Paediatric and Perinatal Epidemiology*, vol 15, no 4, pp 374-8.

Zarb, G. (1993) '"Forgotten but not gone". The experience of ageing with a disability', in S. Arber and M. Evandrou (eds) *Ageing, independence and the life course*, London: Jessica Kingsley Publishers, pp 27–45.

TWO

Time, age and the failing body: A long life with disability

Eva Jeppsson Grassman

Krister was just about to turn 30 when he was interviewed for the first time in 1981. He had become blind a few years earlier as a complication of his juvenile diabetes. He was glowing with youthful enthusiasm. The blindness had changed his life completely, but mainly in a positive sense, he maintained. It had made him break away from his small town life, he said. He had learned new things about himself, and he was looking forward to starting further education and a new career.

Since this first contact, I have followed him for 30 years, through repeated interviews. He has fought for his right to personal development, independence and 'to be like everybody else'. He has moved to different places and has had several jobs. But his life story is also shaped by the many years with chronic illness and disability. It is a story about a trajectory where bodily changes, cumulative impairments and new illness complications have marked his life and where he has repeatedly had to find new adaptive strategies over the years. At the age of not even 50 he was more or less forced into early retirement and this was one of the most painful experiences of his life. His life was lonely when I met him in 1998 and 2006.

When interviewed the last time, in 2011, he was 60. He had then been retired for about 10 years. His disabling conditions limited his life in many ways. He looked back on a life shaped by very particular experiences. Yet somehow he seemed a little more confident than he had been in earlier years, not least concerning his future ability to handle new difficulties.

Introduction

This short excerpt from the biography of a man whose life I have followed for 30 years summarises some of the main themes addressed in this chapter: the long life with progressing disabilities, chronic illness as multiple illnesses, the quest for a fulfilling life in spite of disability, and a lifecourse marked by a work life that was interrupted too early. Yet the excerpt also briefly illustrates the ambiguity of the lifecourse where, perhaps contrary to what might be expected, life prospects seem more optimistic at the age of 60 than at 40 or 50. With the point of departure being the lifecourse perspective, this chapter focuses on the *long life* with disability and on the question of how an early onset of disability shapes life over time and the ageing process. Time is a key concept here, particularly how it is linked to disability, age and ageing. Some questions that will be discussed are: what characterises a long life with disability? How do illness and disability shape the lifecourse? How are we to understand the impact of age and time as themes, and their patterns of change, on the shaping of this process? The discussion builds on results from a truly prospective study in which I have followed a group of chronically ill, visually impaired people for 30 years, through repeated interviews. The framework of the chapter is employment, exit from the labour market and life after retirement. As we shall see, these themes are, to a great extent, influenced by the gradually failing and unpredictable body, which stands out as an over-arching, recurring theme in the interviews over the years, and which is related to the long-term disabling consequences of chronic illness. Time, age and the failing body are central concepts here.

Missing perspectives

As pointed out in Chapter One, prior to this study, relatively little was known about disabled people's lives *over time*, their personal experience of ageing with disabilities and what it means to live with disabilities for many years. Disabled people are often ascribed ambiguous identities, not only with regard to gender but also to age (Jeppsson Grassman, 2001). This may be one explanation for the lack of interest in developing disability research grounded in concepts such as ageing and the lifecourse. Living longer lives and reaching older ages despite disability are also rather recent phenomena for certain groups of disabled people. But another reason for the lack of development of research in this field might be related to the common view of impairment and disability – that they are static conditions (Stiker, 1999). Taking this line, rehabilitation programmes frequently have a 'once and for all' character, based on the assumption that once the individual has reached his 'maximal functional ability', there is no need to worry about additional consequences such as further decline brought about by worsening complications (Stiker, 1999; Williams and Busby, 2000; Jeppsson Grassman, 2001). This view has been common in many countries, not least Sweden. Previous literature focusing on illness and biographical disruption has, by taking this line, tended to concentrate on a short-term perspective in adaptation to illness and disability (Bury, 1982; Jeppsson Grassman, 2001; Taghizadeh Larsson and Jeppsson Grassman, 2012). The perspective of not only *becoming* disabled but of *having to remain* disabled has to date been under-researched.

Furthermore, another perspective that has often been absent in disability research is related to the meaning and impact of *the body and bodily change*. One's experiences of the injured/ill body do not disappear despite measures in the environment or to increase participation, as pointed out by several authors (Hughes and Paterson, 1997; Williams and Busby, 2000; Thomas, 2002; Shakespeare, 2006). Furthermore, social and environmental models of disability have tended to build on assumptions about stable properties in disability and miss out on something that research on chronic illness has unveiled – the changing and unpredictable aspects of the body and the personal experience of an illness trajectory (Williams and Busby, 2000; Jeppsson Grassman, 2005; Taghizadeh Larsson and Jeppsson Grassman, 2012). Chronic illness is the most common cause of disability in the Western world (WHO, 2009). To view ageing as a lifelong process is central in lifecourse research. Yet the body, and conditions such as bodily changes over life, and the ageing body, are themes that are often absent in lifecourse research. This is especially true concerning disabled people and their bodies, particularly from a longitudinal point of view.

Studying lives of disabled people over 30 years

Using a lifecourse perspective in exploring disabled people's lives and ageing implies, as pointed out earlier, that the focus is on the meaning of disability within the *totality of life's dynamics.* Some central concerns are *when* an individual became disabled, *for how long* she or he has had the disability, *how* it has affected the different stages of life and *how old* the individual is at the time of reminiscing on his or her life with disability. The key concepts are *time* and *change*. The *historical time* in which individuals live also has a central significance for this perspective (Giele and Elder, 1998). The cohort concept has a key role here. It refers to individuals who were born at approximately the same time and whose lifecourse is anchored in a common historical time (Alwin and McCammon, 2003), and has been influenced by the same time-bound institutionalised norms (Elder et al, 2003). The relevance of the normative lifecourse concept has, however, been challenged by certain scholars who have argued that, in our time, the lifecourse is increasingly de-institutionalised and characterised by fluid age norms and multiple identities (Hockey and James, 2003; Grenier, 2012). The lifecourse of disabled people may, in its own particular way, be an illustration of this point (Jeppsson Grassman, 2005).

The lifecourse approach is, however, not just a series of theoretical perspectives. It also implies a methodological orientation where the researcher, in a planned way, builds a time dimension into his or her research design and analysis (Giele and Elder, 1998; Jeppsson Grassman, 2001). Thus, the focal point is related to the study of change through repeated data collection *over time* – ranging from one year to many years. This said, it is rather astonishing how rarely prospective approaches are used to explore human change in general and in the area of chronic illness and disability in particular (Jeppsson Grassman, 2012a). There is a tradition for this approach in quantitative research (see Halaby, 2003), but qualitatively oriented, prospective studies are relatively rare and it is only in recent years that such an approach has begun to be developed more systematically in literature on research methods and in empirical studies (Plumridge and Holland, 2003; Sandǎna, 2003; McLeod and Thomson, 2009), although there are some classic prospective studies in which both quantitative and qualitative methods were used (see, for instance, Clausen, 1993). The issues that will be discussed in this chapter have not been a major concern for the researchers in the studies mentioned.

A prospective study of disabled lives

The discussion in this chapter is structured around a study in which a group of participants (14, aged 30-45 at baseline), suffering from chronic illness and severe visual impairment or blindness, were followed over a period of 30 years, through open–ended, qualitative interviews, conducted six times (Jeppsson Grassman, 1986, 2001, 2008, 2012a). The first interview was conducted in 1981, shortly after the onset of their visual impairment. The last interview was conducted in 2011.[1] The purpose was originally to study how the employment and work life of individuals are affected by the onset of severe impairments. The focus, however, was soon widened to include other areas of life, and turned towards the study of how people live for many years with chronic illness and disability and how the change and adaptation process that illness and disability enforces takes shape in different areas of life.

All of the participants, in young adulthood or middle age, have had to live through the great shift in life and the following transition induced by the onset of blindness or severe visual impairment. All of them, for most of their lives, have also had to live with chronic disease in some form. The majority (11) have had diabetes since a young age. Visual impairment is one of several possible complications of this illness. The remaining three people had congenital eye diseases, in one case as part of a rare illness syndrome. With one exception, all participants have subsequently acquired additional disabilities. Thus, dramatic changes have occurred in the lives of the participants, in terms of health and functional capacity. From a long-term perspective it seems clear that the chronic illness is the leitmotif of how life has evolved. In their work life as in their private life, they have been forced to face major transitions. After 30 years, most of them were severely disabled people. At follow–up in 2006, 25 years after the first interview, 10 of the 14 people originally included in the interview group were still alive. The follow–up in 2011 showed that all of those had survived for another five years. The youngest among them were now around 60, and the oldest around 70. The analysis is based on extensive data collected over the 30 years and where the focus was on accounts about present conditions at each interview, on retrospective comparisons and on deliberations about the future.

It is important to note that the participants have grown up, worked and acquired their disabilities under specific historical conditions. They were born in the 1940s and the 1950s. The participants belong to the cohorts who have lived their adult lives in an era when the Swedish modern disability policies were created and implemented. You might say that they belong to the disabled people within their cohorts who were expected to embody modern disability policies, the key concepts of which were integration, normalisation, environmental adjustment and full participation (Jeppsson Grassman, 2001; Gustavsson, 2004). Furthermore, since they were born in the 1940s or in the 1950s, they were young adults in the 1960s and 1970s, but the process of 'becoming old' is connected with the years after the turn of the century. These limits to any generalisations should be kept in mind. On the other hand, whatever their age group and cohort, they have the experience in common with many other disabled people of having *lived with disability for many years*, even if disabled people are by no means a homogeneous group. This also illustrates another important point for this book: there is a great variety of experience among *all* those whom we call 'old' in society, shaped by various conditions throughout their lifecourse.

With a starting point in working life

How does the onset of a severe disability have an impact on the work life of the individual? This was my initial question and the point of departure of my study. Work and work life is a central arena for social belonging, and besides its financial-instrumental importance, it shapes our life in essential ways. The work role is central to the adult part of the lifecourse, and to norms based on the importance of work and employment as a duty, for citizenship, but also for personal development. Norms connected with the work role are strong in most Western countries. This is certainly true for the Nordic countries where 'full employment' has been a strong political goal, which has also permeated disability policies.

Disabled people often have difficulties *getting* jobs, in spite of modern protective legislation, employment and disability policies. Research into this field has often focused on this particular problem. However, it may be just as problematic to be able to *stay* in the labour market, to keep employment, after the onset of impairments and functional loss, *and over the years*.

In the first round of interviews, *in 1981*, of the 14 participants interviewed in the study, 12 had returned to work after occupational rehabilitation. Their employment was protected by laws and regulations passed in the 1970s which had enhanced the chances for disabled people to keep their jobs.[2] These participants were all highly motivated to work, not least because it somehow proved that they were still "the same as before", and "almost like everybody else". Most of the participants were prepared to make far-reaching concessions regarding the qualifications of the work tasks, for example, in order to be able to stay on at work. They belonged to the first generation of disabled people who were accorded a formal right of employment protection. This was a time when Swedish society had high ambitions when it came to full opportunities for work life participation by disabled people. This societal goal also influenced the priorities of the participants. Far-reaching adaptive measures were arranged in the workplace in some of the cases, in order for the participants to be able to carry out their work.

However, in the second round of interviews, *in 1985*, it was already clear to me that the work solutions of 1981 had been fragile constructions for most of the participants. It was hard to keep doing the assigned work tasks over time, due to further functional loss. I realised that what I was actually studying was an ongoing transitional process shaped by the long-term progression of chronic illness and its cumulative disabling consequences. For the participants who had suffered diabetes since childhood, visual impairment was just one of many complications that could afflict them. Some of those participants had not only experienced further loss of eyesight since 1981, they already had additional complications as well. These were not age-related, in the sense that the oldest in the group necessarily had experienced more illness complications than the younger ones. There seemed to be no stability in their work situation, and adaptive measures would repeatedly be necessary. The unpredictability of their chronic illness was now mentioned as stressful to live with by several, and something that influenced how they planned their lives.

A repetitive pattern

After eight years, when interviews were conducted again for a third time, *in 1988-89*, the repetitive character of the adaptive process at work became apparent. Most of the participants had had to face further loss of bodily functioning due to illness complications. Often, there was no preparedness at the workplace for the problems that the cumulative health problems and aggravated impairments entailed. Furthermore, over time, not only did the individual change, but so too did *the environment.* The dimension of time, and change to environment, is seldom recognised in disability research (Jeppsson Grassman, 2005). Yet organisational changes take place, and cutbacks are made, for example, often to the detriment of people such as the participants in the study. The initial enthusiasm among colleagues, seen when the participants first came back to work after rehabilitation, gradually tended to turn into weariness. In the long run, working conditions had become almost unbearable for some of the participants. Being employed was definitely not the same thing as 'full participation'. "It is only now, after all these years that I am realising what it means to live and work as disabled," one participant proclaimed. The *time with disability* and the experience that this had entailed, along with the present conditions, would colour further decisions. Multiple illness complications over the years had made life very exhausting and stressful:

> Lars (50) had always loved his job and continued to work in spite of his blindness. But when interviewed in 1988 he had retired: 'After the leg amputation that I had to go through, it had just become impossible – getting to work, working, getting home, cooking, hygiene, everything took so much more time.'

Some of the participants had already left working life, partly due to this type of problem. They were still young but retired. Never through the whole span of the study would the interviews convey as much distress as at this time. Several of the participants expressed feelings of being very different and remote from people in their own age group. Many were quite apprehensive about their future.

The subsequent interviews over the years would confirm the vulnerability of the participants regarding their chances to stay in employment. This was mainly due to their failing bodies, but also due to failing environments. Yet, as we shall see, *the meaning of work* also seemed to change for some, due to their prior experience of the long time with disability and to their assessment of the future. The case of Karin is an illustration of such a situation:

> She was 40 when interviewed for the first time. Working had always been very important to her and she had been eager to return to work after the onset of her visual impairment. The main reason for this, she later maintained, was that "if I could work, it was a way for me to prove to myself that I was still the same, that I was not only disabled."
>
> When interviewed again, four years later, she had experienced further loss of eyesight, which made her work tasks increasingly difficult for her to master. When interviewed in 1988, she was 48 and had recently retired. Working had become too difficult and her colleagues "were fed up". She had made no further attempts to find another job. Now that she knew how difficult it really was, working was no longer as important to her as it had been earlier, she said. She now had early symptoms of neuropathy, and she had a feeling that "time was running out". "There are other things beside work," she said.

However, age norms and new societal contexts also seemed to play a role. These themes will be discussed in the coming sections. First, the focus is on the bodily consequences of chronic illness over the lifecourse.

Failing bodies: lives with repeated disruptions

When I first met the participants in my study they had recently experienced the onset of visual impairment, in most cases not 'overnight', but through a gradual process in which further loss of eyesight had been feared, expected and yet somehow unexpected when it finally happened (Jeppsson Grassman, 1986). This pattern of changes in bodily function that were both expected and unexpected at the same time would characterise the transitional process, the experience of which the participants would come to share with me over 30 years. Loss of function due to chronic illness often follows a pattern of gradual deterioration, and chronic illness, impairments and disability shape life in particular ways. The onset of chronic illness may occur at any time in the lifecourse. A not very uncommon pattern is chronic illness from birth or childhood where the disabling consequences become apparent and disruptive later – in adulthood. This was the case for all participants in my study. Actually, when I met them for the first time, some of the participants already conveyed the feeling that they had many years of illness to look back on. Retrospectively, in conversations we had in 2006, a similar theme was how the illness had shaped even childhood and youth. Looking back, several of the participants maintained that these phases of their lives, in the 1950s and the 1960s, had been coloured by chronic illness in various ways. Erik (aged 62 in 2006) said he had only been a couple of years old when he fell ill with diabetes:

> 'I have had this illness for almost 60 years, I was so small, of course I had a different upbringing, with all the contact with medical care, and so on.'

Several of the participants pointed out that decisive life choices during their upbringing had been related to the illness. This was the case for Björn (aged 67 in 2006). Major decisions had been shaped by his early awareness of the prognosis of the congenital eye disorder that he shared with other members of his family and which would eventually lead to severe visual impairment:

> 'I had to do everything quickly, before it was too late. I finished my studies quickly, I married and had a child early, and I forced myself to start an early career.'

Recurring illness complications

The visual impairment was *the first major disability* for all of the participants. It would not be the last. The theme of disabling illness complications turned out to be recurring. Most of the participants gave various accounts of repeated illness complications or bodily losses. When interviewed for the third time, in 1988/89, some of the participants had suffered not one 'biographical disruption' (Bury, 1982) but several, that were triggered by kidney failure, heart problems, various symptoms of neuropathy, and so on. The further interviews over the years conveyed a picture in which chronic illness and disablement appeared as parts of an ongoing transitional process. There was no 'once and for all' level of health or functioning.

> Karin, whose exit from work was described in the previous section, had been visually impaired due to diabetes since childhood. After giving up work she had been afflicted with various illness complications. At the time of the interview in 2006 she gave an account of what had happened since we had last met (in 1999). Surgery on her hands and feet had been necessary and she had had by-pass operations on her legs due to poor blood circulation. In passing, she also mentioned

that, three years earlier, she had broken a femur and a shoulder after a fall caused by an insulin coma.

It was also clear, as time passed, that the visual impairment was only one of several illness complications.

'Before, it was all about my visual impairment ... but so much has happened in the last few years: kidney failure last year, and heart failure, my fifth heart attack. I try to think rationally about it, but it is not easy ... I get so upset and worried somehow.' (Krister, aged 55 in 2006)

The body seemed to gradually become run-down and the primary illness was also more difficult to handle:

'Before I had total control,' Erik said. Now, the illness had become very difficult to handle, 'I pass out in comas more often and the emergency services seem to be here to pick me up every so often.' (Erik, aged 62 in 2006)

Time with the illness, time since onset of the visual impairment and time until the next new illness complication represent dimensions of time that were themes in the interviews over the years. The perspective of coping with loss, which seemed to be relevant when describing the lives of several of the participants, could be complemented by the reverse perspective, which was equally relevant: trying to live as ordinary a life as possible *between* losses and disruptions, until the next complication occurred. At no point did the bodily situation seem to 'normalise' in the sense that it was stable. Rather, the 30-year perspective suggested that the participants repeatedly tried to adapt to new levels of health and functioning, only to have to experience a disruption of the acquired new normality due to further illness complications. They seemed to live with double timetables, where complications and losses were both unexpected and expected events. Over the years, most of the participants had gained insight into the probable progression and prognosis of their illness and were well aware of what *could* happen. At the same time, in order to have a tolerable life, they had to live as if that which could happen would not happen, not to them and *at least not now*:

At the time of the first interview in 1981 Christine (40), who had previously lost all eyesight, had just had some surgery which had restored a little eyesight in one eye. Through the years this had been very helpful for her, and 25 years later she told me: 'I can never be sure. I am still doing my little check-up in front of the mirror, first thing in the morning, to make sure I have my little eyesight. And each day I think, now I am safe for *one more day*.' When interviewed again in 2011 she confessed that she still used her 'little check-up routine'.

The analysis gave little support for the argument that ageing or time spent with the illness – and recurring bodily changes – would necessarily make it easier to confront new complications or losses. Rather, it seemed that the risk of experiencing a complication or functional loss as very stressful might be even greater after many years of living with a chronic condition than it had been earlier in the process. Yet at the same time and in the long-term perspective, the analysis indicated that the mere experience of having surmounted repeated disruptive illness complications and survived them might for some individuals, with *age and time*, inspire some confidence regarding their future ability to handle new complications.

Time and a more synchronised lifecourse

The transitional process, caused by illness, seemed to have a repetitive structure. However, the ways in which the disabled individuals assessed and handled key life situations seemed to change over the years, at least in some cases. These ways of handling the situations appeared, on the one hand, to be related to the decreasing possibilities for action that most of the participants now had due to cumulative disabilities. However, on the other hand, it was also evident that the majority of participants had, over time, come to regard important life themes in different ways compared to earlier. Once again the working life was an illustrative example. When interviewed *for the fourth time*, in *1999*, it was quite clear that some of these participants, who had fought to keep their jobs 10 years earlier, had now given up doing so. Their decision was not only a consequence of their experience as employed disabled workers, it also seemed to be linked with *age* and *age norms*: it was perhaps not as important to have a job when you were older, some of the participants said. Not to work when you are 45 makes you very "different", but not to work when you are 55 is "more normal". Changes in society had also taken place. Some of the participants who were 50+ now argued that friends of their age and former colleagues were leaving the labour market or had lost their jobs in the severe recession in the first part of the 1990s. Ten years earlier, several of those interviewed had shared with me their painful feeling of being very different from people of their own age in general and regarding the work role in particular. Now some of them felt more "like everybody else" in certain work–related respects. Time has social connotations, implying norms about what is normal for age, and about the right timing of lifecourse events (Neugarten, 1996). The feeling conveyed now by some of the participants was that they felt more "on time". Their lives were more *synchronised* with social time and age norms, yet some of them were more marked by illness than 10 years earlier.

However, the overall 30-year perspective indicated how age and age norms were intimately, as well as ambiguously, interwoven with the experiences of illness and disability. It seemed hard to separate the meaning of age from the atypical experience of living with disability for many years. The role and importance of age norms also seemed to change over the lifecourse. Furthermore, there was another time dimension that seemed to be handled somewhat differently now, in the late 1990s, compared to earlier, at least in some cases. It was related to the notion of *time left*. Old age and deliberations about time left are sometimes assumed to be connected in an uncomplicated way. Here, over the 30 years, the appearance and subsequent changing patterns of the notion of time left seemed more complex and were related to previous experience, bodily changes, age, but also to peer group comparisons. It was quite clear that the theme of time left had had an impact on the changing adaptive strategies and priorities, not least regarding work.

Time left

The feeling that life is short is one we all have, but it is probably even stronger in people with long-term severe illnesses. All the same, I was surprised when this theme came up in the second round of interviews in 1985, without me having asked anything about it. Several of the participants seemed to have acquired *a new awareness* since we last met about the prospect that the illness would probably shorten their life. An expression that appeared frequently in the interviews at this time was 'time left' and the image of a 'short life'. The painful meaning of this insight was explained by one of the interviewees:

> 'A short life ... I think quite a bit about that ... that I shall have a short life. I have such desire to live that it is hard to accept it.... A short life is a much more distinct thing for me today than six years ago.... Then, I did not have that experience.'

What new experience was that? It was the experience of one's own failing body but also, as it turned out, the experience of *the failing bodies of peers*. After the onset of visual impairment most of the participants had gone away for rehabilitation.[3] Without exception, all of those interviewed who had gone through such a programme highlighted that the most important thing during that time had not been the attainment of new skills, but the social and emotional impact of the experience of meeting visually impaired peers for the first time. In their accounts the positive power of shared experience was a dominating theme in 1981. However, friends and fellow participants in rehabilitation who four years earlier had been described as "being ahead of you" in terms of new skills, were now, in 1985, people who in some cases were ahead of you in a downward-shaped illness trajectory and who, in a particular way, acted as 'door-openers' into a world of decay and possible premature death. "It is like a door that has been opened. You can never forget what is behind that opened door once you have seen it," concluded one participant. Comparisons and identification with the difficult lives of "fellow sufferers" seemed inevitable in certain situations, and the friendships now tended to be associated with loss:

'Some of the people I kept contact with after we finished rehabilitation are already dead,' said Christine (aged 44 in 1985) overwhelmed by sorrow. 'How can anyone expect me not to think about that?'

This awareness of a short life was ever-present for some of the individuals:

'The complications … not knowing how fast they will develop … how many years I have left. Each time I have a new health problem I wonder: how much longer…?' (Uno, aged 42 in 1985)

Others said, they knew "but tried not to think about it too much". A common pattern in 1985 was the opinion that *the scope of planning* ought to be short, since the future was so unpredictable. This limited scope of planning concerned giving up ideas about new 'life projects', new jobs or further education. It seemed meaningless to get a university degree, one of the participants said, since he did not know if he would "ever get to use it". The exit from the labour market was, in some cases strongly influenced by this type of deliberation about the future.

This pattern of 'time left' and of the 'short life' was even stronger, and the theme played a more central role, in the round of interviews *in 1988/89*. At no point in the study did the interviewees spend more time sharing with me their anticipation of a short life and of death than at this time. Their feelings still seemed linked to comparisons with the (short) lifespan of peers. This illustrates the *relational* dimension of time (Jeppsson Grassman, 2012b). The theme of 'time left' was, as before, brought up in connection with life planning: how should one plan life now since it seemed so provisional? One participant, multi-disabled by now and very ill, expressed his views in the following way:

'I view my existence differently now. Maybe I will not wake up tomorrow…. One wakes up and feels happy about that extra day … one does not want to throw it away but really live it to the full.' (Lars, aged 50 in 1988)

For others, who were in a better condition, the situation meant either 'take each day at a time', 'live as intensively as possible *now*', or just 'live on as before', as if severe illness complications would not happen, at least not now.

In *1999* I had followed the group for 18 years. Some participants brought up the theme of a 'short life' once more. However, an interesting discovery was made: This theme was not static, it had changed over time. For a few of the participants this notion was still connected with very strong feelings of uncertainty, which coloured their deliberations about life priorities. For others, and they seemed to be in the majority by this point, the notion of 'time left' seemed to have changed; *The future had expanded* and the horizon of possible planning had been extended. Some of those who had had a very strong feeling of time running out when we last met had actually survived another 10 years. They felt more confident. An overall impression was one of cautious optimism. They had actually survived many of their disabled peers. "Back then, I never thought I would make it," one man said, "so many died."

Even if the interviewees, in terms of their outlook on the future, still had their personal illness trajectory as a reference, the fact that they had survived another 10 years seemed to reassure them about the possibility *of living a longer life than expected*: "Who knows, I might live to be 65," one participant exclaimed. "Living on overtime" seemed to imply that you could be an exception to the rule that was set by some kind of general survival norm discovered by the participants. This idea was associated with how old you could get with severe diabetes, after certain complications, and it was based on general knowledge about the illness that had been acquired through the illness process, and with peers as points of reference. This represents a specific kind of age norm, or 'illness norm', that was not unusual in the interviews.

Survivors

In 2006 and 2011, two of the remaining 11 participants were working part-time, while the others had retired, most of them quite a few years before. The 30-year perspective clearly revealed that the theme 'time left' varied in intensity over time but also between individuals. Some of the interviewees maintained that "things had worked out better than the odds suggested". "The odds" were associated with the state of their body, but also referred to what they knew about the long-term prognosis of their illness. Some were surprised "to have survived the 20th century". One man even maintained that he was older than he "ought to have become", according to the general prognosis of 'people with his illness'. At the same time, it seemed much less appropriate to refer to a 'short life', particularly for those who were now around 65. This old age was viewed as proof of the possibility of a rather *long life* and of the possibility of even having a future. However, the contrary reasoning could also be true. According to some, this 'old age' was an indicator of the fact that life would very soon be over. One could not possibly live much longer with this illness: "*No one* among the people I knew who had this illness ever did that," one participant said.

One strategy was, as it had been all through the process, to ignore the future: "I know things can happen to me … but I try not to think very far ahead … otherwise I would not have the strength to go on," one participant (aged 65) said. Another strategy was to live with 'double agendas', adopting a short- and a long-term planning perspective at the same time. "Who knows, I might be an exception to the rule," one man exclaimed. Being an exception relative to peers meant escaping death for some additional time. Several felt they were *survivors* after all. They were winners of time.

Being old after a long life with disability

What does it mean to 'become and be old', after having survived many years with chronic illness and impairments? For instance, what does it mean, finally, and in spite of everything, to attain an age which, according to societal age norms, is considered to be the 'right time for retirement'? These questions were in focus in the last two rounds of interviews, and particularly in 2011. The participants were aged around 60-70 then. The questions have to do with a more fundamental question of whether this stage is characterised by a 'double difference', or if life has gradually 'normalised' with age in that one's life begins to look more like that of other older people. Perhaps it is a question of both. For a few, life seemed to have become more like that of other retired people who had passed the 'normal' time of retirement. However, life for most participants now seemed less shaped by age norms than by the state of their body. They were actually not very old, chronologically speaking, yet their level of bodily functioning was "like that of an 85-year-old", as one participant expressed it. To still successfully manage everyday life – to retain the ability to go out and to participate in any kind of social activity, for example – came up as an important theme of normality. One aspect of a theme that might be called *body time* suggested an important time dimension related to this: everyday life and any participation took much more time to handle now due to the cumulative disabilities and to the failing body.

While a few of the participants with reasonably good health managed to live rather active 'third-age lives', and be more like "any retired person", the multiple disabilities, in most cases, created very restricted lives that were more concordant with the concept of 'fourth-age lives', in spite of their relatively young age. In 2011, the lives of the participants varied; however, this was not only due to the degree of illness and disability and to resources in the environment, but also depended on important decisions taken earlier and throughout the lifecourse that had left imprints. Several had refrained from having children for fear of congenital risks connected with their illness. Some had always lived alone, one reason being that they had not wanted to "saddle the burden of care" that they had foreseen would come "on to a partner". Loneliness had been a theme in the interviews off and on, over the years. It was quite obvious from early on that those participants who lived with someone had a freer and more flexible life than those who lived alone. In spite of the presence of formal care and support systems, family proved to be crucial if one was to have a reasonable "space" in one's daily life as a severely disabled person – and this was particularly apparent at this late stage of the illness trajectory. Autonomy had been a key theme through the years, and in many ways an unattainable goal, but *with age* it had become easier to ask for help:

> 'I always found it difficult to ask for help ... but it is easier now, at 70 than it was at 50.' (Christine, aged 70 in 2011)

This seemed to have to do with age norms. Yet if age norms had been important in certain situations 15 years earlier, chronological age no longer meant much, and general age norms meant less and less, according to some participants. "I have been retired for such a long time now that the age for retirement and old age has no meaning to me," one participant maintained. Another participant said that he was now so ill and confined to his home that he "no longer had any opportunity to compare [himself] to anything or anybody". After many years of retirement, and with extensive disabilities, some participants seemed to live rather detached from "the vibrations of everyday life". A few, however, found their age and the norms connected with it helpful. One of them was Björn, a participant who had actually managed to work until the age of 65:

> He was a person who had had high expectations at work, not least concerning his own performance. But his work life had become marked by disappointments, partly due to his visual impairment. It had been a relief, he said, to be able to retire, and 'become just a normal old man'. Finally, at 65, and after all these years, he had been able to make himself use the white stick. It gave him a kind of authority when he was out walking and, given his age, he felt he had a full right to use it.

Age in his case had had a normalising function. For others, the state of the body meant more, and the meaning of age seemed more than ever overshadowed by the impact of the long time with illness and disabling conditions:

> 'I don't think about my age very often anymore. What I think about is that I have had diabetes for 55 years now … that I think about.' (Christine, aged 70 in 2011)

To be "an old diabetic" or "an old visually impaired person", expressions used by the participants, did not have as much to do with chronological age as with the number of years with the illness or impairment. An overall impression from this last round of interviews was that the participants now had a freer, perhaps more detached, attitude to age and age norms than before.

An existential theme that came up over the years was related to the question of how to keep one's spirits up – *in spite of everything*. An interesting observation was that the participants, during the last interview, in 2011, expressed more optimism in this regard than had been seen in some of the earlier interviews. They all lived with the existential dilemma of having to face the unpredictability of the illness, the body and the uncertain future. Yet some of the participants expressed more confidence in their own ability to cope with the recurring difficulties. Life is complex and the lifecourse does not necessarily always have a simple downward course, even for severely ill people. There was a kind of serenity in their accounts, as if the participants could take comfort from in the fact that they had, after all, survived *all these years*, and *attained old age*. Some participants conveyed the idea that "the worst was behind" them. They were living on *overtime*, some of them proclaimed, and they were actually exceptions in many ways. "I have no future," one participant said, "but it does not matter anymore." "The now" was what counted.

Conclusion

This chapter has focused on what it means to live a long life with disabilities, and how continuous illness complications and various dimensions of time may have an impact on this experience. Illness and disability shape the lifecourse of the disabled person in very marked and particular ways, especially due to the transitional character of the chronic illness that is often the primary cause of impairments. As seen in this chapter, living a long life with disability often means living with *a gradually failing and unpredictable body*, around which it is difficult to build stable solutions. This is the key theme in my study. It implies living permanently with an uncertain future, which in turn entails particular experiences that have an impact on the lived experience of later life. To live and age with disability, for severely disabled people, often signifies not being 'on time' in various situations: leaving work life too early, having the impression that it would be too late to get higher education, needing extensive help far too young, and so on. From the 30-year perspective, it was clear that age norms often seemed to function as markers of difference for the participants, yet at certain times they could also be supportive and have a normalising function. However, age as such seemed to be of subordinate importance. Instead, the extent of illness complications, and embodied time, played a decisive role. At times, the participants seemed to replace age norms with *illness norms*, with reference to disabled peers. *Time left* was a key theme in the lives of the participants, but it varied in intensity and shape over the years and in relation to ageing and old age. An overall conclusion is that the temporal dimensions of the lifecourse that has been studied over 30 years are in fact complex: time with illness and disability, age, 'time left' and relational time − all are interwoven in complex ways and according to changing patterns in the studied processes, which were shaped by illness complications and gradual functional loss.

At the same time, it is important to note that, while it is the phenomenon of the long life with disability that has been explored and from which the conclusions are drawn, the study is anchored in a specific time. The people followed for 30 years in my study have lived and grown old in post-war Sweden, and with serious chronic illness, mainly diabetes. This raises questions to be explored further, not only about long lives with other illnesses and disabilities, but also about a long life with disability in other contexts of time and place. There are similarities but there may also be differences (Taghizadeh Larsson and Jeppsson Grassman, 2012).

The focus in this chapter has been on the themes of time, age and body. Other themes in the extensive data that were collected for my study were thus left aside or only touched on. One such theme is family relations over the lifecourse.

The meaning of autonomy, integrity and care turned out to be other themes of key importance in the long lives with disability. Some of these themes will be elaborated on in some of the coming chapters, but from other perspectives.

Notes

[1] Interviews were conducted in 1981, 1985, 1988/89, 1999, 2006 and 2011.

[2] The 1974 Act on Protection of Employment (amended in 1982) was one such law.

[3] At that time in Sweden, in the early 1980s, rehabilitation for severely disabled people who wished to return to work was still organised in the form of full-week programmes running from six months to more than a year, within the premises of boarding school facilities that one "went away to".

References

Alwin, D.F. and McCammon, R.J. (2003) 'Generations, cohorts and social change', in J.T. Mortimer and M.J. Shanahan (eds) *Handbook of the life course*, New York: Kluwer Academic, pp 23-49.

Bury, M. (1982) 'Chronic illness as biographical disruption', *Sociology of Health and Illness*, vol 4, no 2, pp 167-82.

Clausen, J.A. (1993) *American lives: Looking back at the children of the great depression*, New York: Free Press.

Elder, G.H. Jr, Kirkpatrick Johnson, M. and Crosnoe, R. (2003) 'The emergence and development of life course theory', in J.T. Mortimer and M.J. Shanahan (eds) *Handbook of the life course*, New York: Kluwer Academic, pp 3-19.

Giele, J.Z. and Elder, G.H. (1998) 'Life course research: development of a field', in J.Z. Giele and G.H. Elder (eds) *Methods of life course research: Qualitative and quantitative approaches*, London: Sage Publications, pp 5-27.

Grenier, A. (2012) *Transitions and the lifecourse: Challenging the constructions of 'growing old'*, Bristol: The Policy Press.

Gustavsson, A. (ed) (2004) *Delaktighetens språk* [*The language of participation*], Lund: Studentlitteratur.

Halaby, C.N. (2003) 'Panel models for the analysis of change and growth', in J.T. Mortimer and M.J. Shanahan (red) *Handbook of the life course*, New York: Kluwer Academic, pp 503-27.

Hockey, J. and James, A. (2003) *Growing up and growing old: Ageing and dependency in the life course*, London: Sage Publications.

Hughes, B. and Paterson, K. (1997) 'The social model of disability and the disappearing body: towards a sociology of impairment', *Disability & Society*, vol 12, no 3, pp 325-40.

Jeppsson Grassman, E. (1986) *Work and new visual impairment: A study of the adaptive process*, Stockholm Studies in Social Work 2, Stockholm: Liber.

Jeppsson Grassman, E. (2001) 'Tid, tillhörighet och anpassning. Kronisk sjukdom och funktionshinder ur ett livsloppsperspektiv' ['Time, belonging and adaptation. Chronic illness from a life course perspective'], *Socialvetenskaplig Tidskrift*, vol 8, no 4, pp 306-26.

Jeppsson Grassman, E. (2005) 'Tid, rum, kropp och livslopp. Nya perspektiv på funktionshinder' ['Time, space, body and life course. Disability from new perspectives'], in E. Jeppsson Grassman and L.-Ch. Hydén (eds) *Kropp, livslopp och åldrande: Några samhällsvetenskapliga perspektiv* [*Body, life course and ageing: Some social perspectives*], Lund: Studentlitteratur, pp 19-52.

Jeppsson Grassman, E. (ed) (2008) *Att åldras med funktionshinder* [*Ageing with disability*], Lund Studentlitteratur.

Jeppsson Grassman, E. (2012a)) 'Å studere funksjonshemmedes liv over lang tid: Noen refleksjoner omkring aldrende forskere og informanter' ['To study disabled lives over many years. Reflections over the relationship between ageing scholars and interviewees'], in K. Thorsen and E. Jeppsson Grassman (eds) *Livsløp med funksjonshemning. Perspektiver og tilnærminger* [*Life course and disability*], Oslo: Cappelen Akademisk, pp 289-307.

Jeppsson Grassman, E. (2012b) 'Chronic illness, awareness of death and the ambiguity of peer identification', in D. Davies and C. Park (eds) *Emotion, identity and death: Mortality across disciplines*, Farnham: Ashgate, pp 15-28.

McLeod, J. and Thomson, R. (2009) *Researching social change: Qualitative approaches*, London: Sage Publications.

Neugarten, B.L. (ed) (1996) *The meaning of age: Selected papers of Bernice Neugarten*, Chicago, IL: University of Chicago Press.

Plumridge, L. and Holland, J. (2003) 'Hindsight, foresight and insight: the challenges of longitudinal qualitative research', *International Journal of Social Research Methodology*, vol 6, no 3, pp 233-44.

Sandåna, J. (2003) *Longitudinal qualitative research: Analyzing change through time*, New York and Oxford: Alta Mira Press.

Shakespeare, T. (2006) *Disability rights and wrongs*, London: Routledge.

Stiker, H.-J. (1999) *A History of Disability*, Ann Arbor: University of Michigan Press.

Taghizadeh Larsson, A. and Jeppsson Grassman, E. (2012) 'Bodily changes among people with physical impairments and chronic illness – biographical disruption or normal illness?', *Sociology of Health and Illness*, vol 34, no 8, pp 1156-1169.

Thomas, C. (2002) 'Disability theory: key ideas, issues and thinkers', in C. Barnes, M. Oliver and L. Barton (eds) *Disability studies today*, Cambridge: Polity Press, pp 38-58.

WHO (World Health Organization) (2009) *Global health risks: Mortality and burden of disease attributable to selected major risks*, Geneva: WHO.

Williams, G. and Busby, H. (2000) 'The politics of disabled bodies', in S.J. Williams, J. Gabe and M. Calnan (eds) *Health, medicine and society: Key theories, future agendas*, London: Routledge, pp 169-85.

THREE

Disability, identity and ageing

Lotta Holme

'In contrast to previous living conditions, we now gain access to normal ageing.' (Oscar, 62 years old)

Introduction

In this chapter I explore from a lifecourse perspective how important leading activists of the modern Swedish disability movement regard their ageing and later life. More specifically, I focus on how a special group of disabled people experience ageing and later life in light of the modern history of disability and disability politics in which they have actively participated (see also Campbell and Oliver, 1996; Hugemark and Roman, 2007; Symeonidou, 2009). I discuss the importance of identity as a disabled person and how this is socially shaped and described.

Aim and questions

The aim of this chapter is to examine perspectives and experiences of ageing in relation to what can be seen as a so-called normal lifecourse (Priestley, 2003). The concept of a political lifecourse perspective is introduced in order to create an understanding of the links between experiences of disability, activism and a normal lifecourse (Andrews, 2007). The main questions are: how have the political and personal standpoints that disabled people have taken throughout their lives shaped their views of ageing and later life? How does a disability identity have an impact on these views? How does this group reflect on discrimination and ageism? Finally, do they think that ageing and later life will be different for them and for other disabled people compared to non-disabled people?

The historical context is that disability policy progressed and identity politics were developed by the disability rights movement in Western countries' welfare states from the 1950s onwards. The point of departure for this chapter is the fact that, now, for the first time in history, a generation of people who have lived a long life with disability can look back on an important era of disability policy development in which they have participated and have been pioneers themselves.

This chapter builds on biographical interviews with eight disabled people who have lived for many years with disability. What is special about this group is that they are all devoted, well-known and successful disability activists. They have had (and some still have) leading positions in different parts of the modern Swedish disability movement, and over the years they have developed strong disability identities. An implication of this is that the group in question has more reasons than most other people to explore and profoundly reflect on disability issues, both in their personal lives as well as in connection with their positions in the movement (see also Campbell and Oliver, 1996; Andrews, 2007).

The informants have different types of impairments, mainly visual impairments, polio, arthritis and mobility impairments. At the time of the interviews the informants were 58-70 years old. In the study they are called Elizabeth, Eric, Frank, George, Harry, Maria, Oscar and William. The interviews were conducted from 2008 to 2011 and lasted from one to two hours. The interviews were recorded, transcribed and analysed from a biographical lifecourse perspective.

I begin with an introduction of a political lifecourse perspective and the concept of a collective political disability identity. This is followed by and closely linked to a description of the story of the disability rights movement and disability politics and their increasing impact over the last 40 years of disability history in Sweden. This story emerges in the course of the eight interviews. After this, I discuss perspectives and experiences of disability and ageing, based on an analysis of the attitudes and experiences of ageing expressed by the informants. The so-called normal lifecourse and double discrimination are central concepts in the following sections, as well as ideas of what later life should be like. The chapter is rounded off by some remarks on the importance of a political lifecourse perspective, a discussion of a collective disability history identity, and finally, how a deeper understanding can be developed of disabled people's experience and reflections on their own and others' ageing and later life.

Narratives of identity

The interest in biographical methods and research on stories (so-called narrative research) has increased in the past few years (Andrews, 2007). Historians and sociologists, for example, have begun to reconstruct human experience (Shakespeare, 1996). In fact, so many studies have been carried out and articles published that some of the leading researchers in the field want to call this phenomenon the biographical turn in social science research (Chamberlayne et al, 2004). Andrews (2007, p 10) shares this opinion: 'Stories and storytelling are no longer the province of the playroom, but rather are increasingly regarded as an important arena for serious scholarly investigation'. She calls such life stories narratives of identity. In my study, on which this chapter is based, interviews were carried out that focused on stories about the political process over a long period of time.

One special topic in biographical research is *stories* about political activism and identity politics. Narratives of political activism often include how a person looks upon him or herself in relation to other activists, and whom to consider as members of one's own group. The stories also contain narratives on policy and political change. *Identity* becomes something that is constantly negotiated and renegotiated in discussions with others, co-thinkers as well as political opponents. Such themes are examples of what could be seen as important building blocks of such stories. Andrews (2007) discusses methods and perspectives in political biographical research based on life stories, and claims that such stories are always important for the shaping of a collective and national identity. Those stories thus have both a political/collective and a personal dimension (Gullette, 2003). In my data, as will be shown in the analysis, this stands out very clearly.

So, closely linked to life stories and a political lifecourse perspective is the concept of political identity. A person's life story, his or her history, is crucial to his or her identity (Andrews, 2007). Andrews (2007, p 11) argues: 'Narratives provide a very rich basis from which to explore political identities; critically, what an individual or a community chooses to tell about themselves is intricately tied to how they construct their political identities.' Individual and collective memories are negotiated in between the stories of history and one's own life. Shakespeare claims that 'Identity is about stories, having the space to tell them, and an audience which will listen' (1996, p 113). In this chapter, a political lifecourse perspective is used as a frame for understanding political activism and identity politics with a specific focus on disability policy and disability as a social identity. The next section focuses on disability as a political identity based on common narratives of the history of the disability rights movement.

The story of the modern disability rights movement in Sweden

The history of the modern disability rights movement in Sweden has been reproduced many times and in different contexts, both orally and in writing (see, for example, HCK, 1992; Lindberg, 2006; Holme, 2008; Sjöberg, 2010). A relatively coherent story was also presented in the interviews on which this description is based. All of the interviewed have a strong historical awareness and have themselves taken part in the shaping of the disability movement's history, which therefore becomes both individual and public. The disability biographical perspective becomes evident in the historical images of the disability movement's ups and downs.

Normalisation principle and A Society for All

The modern Swedish disability movement's origins go back to the normalisation principle of the 1960s (Nirje, 2003), even though none of the eight informants in my study felt very comfortable with the concept. George, one of the informants, said that the normalisation principle came from the outside: "This was the professional way of looking at us. It was we who would be normalised. And our living conditions." Another of the informants, Maria, claimed that there was nothing wrong with the normalisation principle, really, but it felt more natural to formulate this principle in terms of striving for a life like most others, with "family life, schooling and all areas of life." "We wanted to be a part of society," Oscar concluded, "as citizens with equal rights and obligations as everyone else."

The great breakthrough for the disability movement came in the 1970s. According to Maria, it then became a movement with strong ideas, to be compared to other social movements. In 1972 the Handikappförbundens Centralkommitté (Disability Federation Central Committee) introduced a joint disability programme, called A Society for All, and 1972 is seen as a milestone in the Swedish disability movement and in the disability history of Sweden. The Committee organised collaboration between a number of the largest and most influential disability organisations from 1964-93. As early as the 1960s, the concept of disability in official documents and legal texts included some social model elements, and in the programme A Society for All it was claimed that society and the environment should be designed according to the needs of all citizens. It was not enough to bring the individual to society; Society must also be made accessible. George put it like this:

> 'We took a giant step forward in the early 70s when the focus shifted from the individual person to be helped, strengthened and rehabilitated, and so it is of course important that this will continue. But it's also like this: society must be made accessible, so that it suits those of us living with disabilities. It was a shift in focus.'

The importance of a common concept of disability

What George talks about here is the main idea, the environmentally relative disability concept or, as Shakespeare (2004, 2006) calls it, the Nordic relational model (Holme, 2006; See also Chapter One), which managed to unite quite different groups of disabled people in a joint political programme (see also Symeonidou, 2009). The concept emphasised the importance of the environment for the creation of disability, without sacrificing or ignoring different groups or individuals' points of view or special interests. One of the informants, Eric, compared this to earlier periods of time when "there was talk *about* the handicapped", and he argued that "disability is not a physical, but a social phenomenon", which is a prerequisite for the relative concept of disability. He said:

> 'We were identified as handicapped, and objectified as people with disabilities, but the concept was not yet so, that was something that was very important to me, to highlight the question of our human identity. The handicap is not really in my personality, in our persons, but it is in the surrounding circumstances. You knew when the relative approach was accepted it was controversial. For the first time I think

that one can say that disability issues were raised with a coherent political viewpoint.'

Earlier studies of narratives show that common concepts and ideas are of political importance for successful identity politics, and the informants in this study shared this opinion (Andrews, 2007). Symeonidou (2009) has studied expressions of the disability experience of some of the leading activists of the Cypriot disability movement. In Cyprus, the disability groups' affiliations were developed based on specific disabilities and diagnoses, but no overall disability movement has grown strong, and there is therefore no availability to a collective disability identity. The main reason for this, Symeonidou (2009) claims, is that the disability movement lacks theoretical concepts and perspectives: 'Linked to the absence of a theoretical framework that could guide disability politics in Cyprus is the absence of a collective identity' (2009, p 29). The Nordic countries, she says, have the environmentally relative concept of disability, and in the UK, the social model serves as a theoretical superstructure. Symeonidou shows that political movements must be placed in a social, historical and cultural context to be fully understood and reasonably described.

A collective story of disability rights movement history

In the UK a collective consciousness of disabled people arose during the 1970s and 1980s (Campbell and Oliver, 1996). This awareness includes the *history* of the disabled as an essential part. Campbell and Oliver (1996) put together a mix of economic, social and political observations and theories as well as individual and collective experiences of disabled people. The purpose of this was to describe and discuss the modern British disability rights movement's struggle for an equal society by giving disabled people who were committed to the movement an opportunity to express their views on issues relating to participation, citizenship, civil rights and political awareness. According to Campbell and Oliver (1996), a disability consciousness that takes both individual and collective expressions in a new and modern social movement is a prerequisite for success: 'What, in our view, constitutes the most significant issue that makes new social movements ... [is] that of transforming the individual and collective consciousness of the membership' (Campbell and Oliver, 1996, p 123). A collective disability history narrative is seen to be a key element in this consciousness (Barnes and Mercer, 2010). The British disability movement is described as a political and social success, even though Campbell and Oliver (1996) realise that much political work remains to be done to increase disability awareness, especially from a global perspective.

The Swedish collective history of the disability movement always includes the environmental relative disability concept, de-institutionalisation and the struggle against charity, the radicalisation of the disability movement and the emergence of modern disability politics, especially the two disability rights laws: the 1993 Act concerning Support and Service for Persons with Certain Functional Impairments and the 1993 Assistance Compensation Act. Sometimes the narratives also highlight the Independent Living Movement, and international work on disability issues. Disability research is occasionally mentioned as important for improving disability issues and their status in society (Holme and Olsson, 2001; Holme, 2006; Lindberg, 2006; Holme, 2008). The informants Elizabeth and Oscar believe that disability research has been of great importance in this respect, while George and Frank consider research to be far too limited when it comes to content and scope.

Institutions

Institutions for the disabled are the starting point in the story of the disability movement, as it is usually told. It is against this often unmentioned background that the development of participation in society is described. One could say that the main driving force of the modern disability policy is disabled people trying to get included in different contexts, from which they were previously excluded (see also HCK, 1992; Lindberg, 2006; Holme, 2008; Sjöberg, 2010). Maria mentions de-institutionalisation, but the focus of the collective story is on the opportunities to shape one's own life, to get self-determination, to avoid paternalism and "wiseacres who put me on a predictable way from birth to grave," as Frank put it.

Charity

In line with the struggle for independence a very critical view of charity was expressed by the informants and also in written narratives (see, for example, HCK, 1992; Lindberg, 2006; Holme, 2008; Sjöberg, 2010). Oscar said that the meaning of charity was discrimination, stigmatisation and humiliation. We want "our rights to be jointly financed by the taxes", he argued. Charity was, said Maria, a way to make discrimination permanent, "where the person who gives also determines the conditions". "Charity-thinking means that there is someone else who has control over help and support," Elizabeth said. It counteracted autonomy and independence, and it put disabled people in a disadvantaged position.

The negative attitude towards charity is understandable in light of the struggle for the right to a personal assistant, a political reform that takes a unique and symbolic position in the history of the Swedish disability movement. For the informants interviewed, the 1993 Assistance Compensation Act was the single most important disability political reform to have been achieved in modern times. Maria believed that it was a "very important reform" and Elizabeth thought that it "marks a new approach to disabled people and disability policy."

Labour market and accessibility

However, there are at least two areas in disability politics that the disability movement and society had conspicuously failed to change, according to the interviewees. One area was the labour market, to which disabled people had never managed to gain full entry, and the second failure concerned accessibility to buildings, transport and so on. Both areas were seen by the informants as essential for participation in society. Full citizenship, with its rights and its obligations, was impossible as long as the labour market was closed due to inaccessibility. Eric described the labour market as "a total failure":

> 'If we take the state authorities, first, they have the responsibility to adjust buildings and workplaces to disabled people; it is actually a mission they have but they do nothing. They have a responsibility to fix their workplaces in such ways that you can be there and do meaningful work, but they do nothing about this. They prefer gorgeous old houses with all sorts of strange things in the planning, so someone with a disability cannot work there.'

The disability movement's history can be said to be both personal and collective, and it provides an opportunity for positive identification. As has been pointed out, it encompasses the injustices, the struggles and the successes that will nourish disability policy in the future. It is partly from the historical narratives of life in isolation and poverty of the institutions that disability activism derives its power. The personal life stories intertwine with the general picture. The stories of progress made are important as a source of inspiration for the resistance encountered (see, for example, HCK, 1992; Lindberg, 2006; Holme, 2008; Sjöberg, 2010).

Disability identity

The collective history of disability is an important component of a disability identity. The interviews with this special group of people, who for many years have had leading positions in the Swedish disability movement, show no distinction between disability history and the disability movement's history. To the informants it was the same thing. It was from the many years of ups and downs that one could gain strength and energy. The historical perspective contributes in various ways, and has the function of bringing respect for the struggle of the past and giving hope for future victories. The informants have all been involved in the modern disability movement and the emergence of disability politics. Personal memories and experiences were included and interwoven into the collective story. Disability history thus provides energy for a collective disability identity, and from this perspective it can be argued that there is indeed such an identity, along with other individual and social positions.

Disability identity is complicated and therefore challenging to describe and discuss. It has personal as well as collective dimensions, and is constantly negotiated and renegotiated in social life. But at the same time a disability identity may be both strong and consistent. One of the building blocks of disability identity is political activism; one is a common picture of disability history.

Hugemark and Roman (2007) found in a study that disability organisations in Sweden cultivate the idea of a dichotomy that is said to exist between non–disabled and disabled people. Therefore, many members are not content to be represented by a person with no experience of living with disability. Hugemark and Roman (2007) compare this with the British disability movement, which from the 1960s has changed from just providing support for people with disabilities to *include* disabled people (see also Barnes and Mercer, 2010). However, Hugemark and Roman (2007) conclude that a uniform collective disability identity is difficult to find in Sweden, and they refer to the conflicts and contradictions that exist within the organisations. One reason for different opinions is the various kinds of disabilities and diagnoses, but the differences are complex and also relate to 'questions of group identity (who are "we"?), claims for justice (what do we want?), and representation (who can legitimately speak for us?)' (Hugemark and Roman, 2007, p 43).

An identity can be said to consist of several components, some of which are subject to constant renegotiation of social life, while others are more persistent over time (Shakespeare, 1996; Gullette, 2003). Identity is built up, assigned or adopted by an individual in relation to a social categorisation, and it is also related to age and age norms (Hockey and James, 2003; Jenkins, 2008; Närvänen, 2009). It is obvious that all eight informants in this chapter, disability activists as they are, have an identity strongly associated with and linked to their involvement in disability issues. This leads the discussion to how life stories on disability on the one hand, create and on the other, are created by, a strong identification (Shakespeare, 1996). Therefore, the main questions are how disabled people base their identity on being active in the disability movement and in disability policy, how an identity as a disabled person is created by narratives of disability history and how a modern disability identity is described and perceived.

Shakespeare has discussed and problematised disability identity (Shakespeare, 1993, 1996, 2004) and he believes, like Campbell and Oliver (1996), that there are a number of different possible identities and social positions, which are formed in the intersection between an individual's social experience of disability and external conditions and processes. Shakespeare argues that disabled people's narratives about their lives and experiences together create a collective story, which provides identification, and he claims that 'identity is an aspect of the stories we tell ourselves, and to others' (Shakespeare, 1996, p 95). 'It cannot be denied', he concludes, that 'disability is a very strong identity' (p 109), but there is a set of different identities. People can identify with more social categories than one, and Shakespeare (1996) notes that some disabled people do not want to embrace an identity as a disabled person, but prefer and strive to remain outside the collective story. Priestley (2003) argues that disabled people can choose among several different identities; The modern disability movement has expanded the concept of identity through cultural and social activities.

However, according to Shakespeare (1993, 1996), there is a risk that a person can be attributed a negative identity as a disabled person (see also Jenkins, 2008) because of the dominance of the medical model, and the discrimination resulting from this model. A counterforce is created when disabled people organise and identify themselves in a positive way, politically, socially and culturally, and making this happen is the most important task for the disability movement, as Shakespeare sees it (1996, p 101):

> The disability movement provides the collective context for political identification; it involves processes which challenge views of disabled people as incapable, powerless and passive; And it establishes disabled people as the experts on disability and disabled people's definitions as the most appropriate approaches to disability.

Experiences of disability, ageing and later life

In previous sections of this chapter I have shown the importance of a disability identity to the informants interviewed in this study. I have argued that the historical awareness and pragmatic consensus on disability concepts unites disabled people in the disability movement. In this section I discuss from a political lifecourse perspective how political and personal standpoints affect attitudes of ageing and later life. The implications of identity, disability experiences and political views are claimed to be important for a deeper understanding of this special group's reflection on, for instance, ageism (see also Jönson and Taghizadeh Larsson, 2009).

Krekula (2006) argues that the discussion taking place within social gerontological research shows two main positions regarding the perceptions of ageing in the sense of getting old. Krekula (2006) refers to Biggs, who has described these key positions in several articles and who argues that these positions in research must be considered simultaneously. One position is based on ageing, physical decline and social isolation, and is associated with ageism, and the other advocates ageing that involves personal development (see also Chapter Five and Biggs, 2001).

Krekula (2006) also discusses research which, in different ways, illustrates the experiences of ageing. According to Krekula's discussion, experiences of ageing are highly subjective and can be divided into at least three categories: the first is how an individual experiences his or her own ageing; The second is how an individual experiences others' ageing; And finally, how society regards a person who is old.

Attitudes to ageing and later life

One of the key questions I asked in the interviews was how the informants looked on their own and others' ageing, and how they imagined later life compared to those who lacked experience of living with disability. "It is an important question you ask" Oscar said. "I have been thinking a lot about the effects of ageing, because it affects me. It affects us all." Ageing in itself, in the sense of growing old, was described by Eric and George as something that offered opportunities for development and fulfilment and to continue the disability policy commitment. The increased restrictions that loss of functions implied should not be seen as obstacles. These could be compensated for in various ways, such as personal assistance or technical aids (see also Holme, 2008). Elizabeth and Frank, however, were more pessimistic and saw ageing and disability as mutually reinforcing. Elizabeth often felt "sorrow for lost functions" and was discouraged by these thoughts. Frank developed strategies on how to prepare himself mentally for his later life and for the loss of identity that he believed it would entail. He declared:

> 'It becomes more difficult in economic terms when you get old, but also emotionally, because you will get the feeling that you are of no use to society, that you aren't worth anything. These reflections increase the feeling of alienation which I already have.'

Indeed, ageing affects all human beings, but could it be *fair*? Can disability be fully compensated for? Does age affect everyone in the same way, or does it differ between disabled and non-disabled people? There were different opinions about whether the effects of ageing were fair or not among the informants. Disabled people, of course, compare themselves with people of their own biological/ chronological age. To 'suffer' from ageing which does not distinguish disabled people from most others would then be a fair form of ageing.

The view that ageing for disabled people should be fair and should not differ from the ageing of non-disabled people was expressed in some of my interviews. The starting point for such an approach is the two Acts of 1993, that is, the right laws whose intention is that with the help of a personal assistant, a person with severe disabilities can live like most other people. Since the introduction of this law, it has been seen as possible even for disabled people to grow old like other people. This may seem an idealistic position, but it is quite common among disability activists; between a disabled person and a non-disabled person there should be no differences in terms of opportunities for and obstacles to a normal lifecourse involving family, schooling, work and later life. This approach to disability and ageing could be described as compensatory. Oscar declared:

> 'My firm opinion is that it shouldn't be any different [between ageing for disabled and non-disabled] ... in contrast to previous living conditions, we can now gain access to normal ageing.... With these conditions [personal assistance] I age like other people.'

The normative perspective, the principle that there should be no difference between the ageing of non-disabled and disabled people, was thus represented among my interviewees, combined with the view that old age should be a very active and rich part of life. Some of the informants still had no personal experience of their own ageing, but expressed ideas about how it might be and how it should be in later life. In this context, they mentioned that later life for disabled people should be like that of most others, and that there were no real obstacles to old age being an active and outgoing time. It was society that created opportunities or barriers for participation and equality, and participation in society and politics was crucial for self-realisation, even in old age. Oscar explained:

> 'My disabilities are compensated for by the personal assistance, and I can live like others of the same age, that is, have a life like many elderly people in Sweden today, who live as active pensioners, often up to 85 years old – and even into the 90s.'

Such an approach sees disability as a static condition, as something received earlier in life, clearly defined and not changing. It is a consequence of 'passed illnesses'. This approach assumes normal ageing and ageing not affected by, or even in relation to, disability. In this context, one could also identify a stereotype, one of the interviewed said, namely, that disabled people were seen as physically weaker than others. There were examples of this, but there were also examples of the opposite; That disabled people were basically physically strong.

But the experiences of ageing were also described, for example, by the expression that "age takes its toll". These views assumed that ageing meant that you got ailments and became frail, that you could not participate in society and family life as you used to, and that ageing thus involved a gradual increase in restrictions and obstacles. Elizabeth expressed this as follows:

> 'Ageing takes its toll physically in a faster way for those who have had reduced functionality for many years compared to others.... Those who have impaired body functions often live with very thin margins.... A small decline could have significant consequences.... This is precisely what happens when we age.'

This approach was based on the informants' own experiences of various body functions disappearing due to age, and that these processes were intimately linked to disability. A long life with impairments definitely left its mark. For example, repetitive strain injury occurs as a result of long-term compensations in various ways for reduced functionality. Another concern was that independence would be further reduced and that dependence on others would increase.

Eric thought that so-called 'normal' age ailments would be added to those he already had. Some impairments suffered earlier in life had late effects, and "the usual ageing process comes earlier and faster". This argument was based on the recognition that disability was not something static or something that could be regarded as a given component. The 'old' disability manifested itself in different ways and affected the ageing process, and the whole process was not fully comparable to the ageing that affected non-disabled people.

George made an interpretation that was basically the same, but had a more dramatic approach. He believed that disabled people suffered far more by loss of functions, caused by 'normal' ageing, than non-disabled. He said:

> 'The fear of other impairments is probably genuine, deeply human, and affect us all.... We, disabled people, are also afraid. Think of me; being blind, I would be far more vulnerable if my hearing disappeared too.'

Ageing had thus increased problems and complications for disabled people compared with non-disabled people. A different approach was expressed by Frank, who said that disabled people could be better equipped mentally to handle additional disabilities than most others. He put it this way:

> '... it is clear that if you have lived with disability ... and get other ailments, then you are a little better prepared for what disability means, for all you have to deal with, and understand that you can no longer do what you did and how roles must be affected. You recognise the new restrictions in the old ones.... You have armed yourselves better, you could say....'

Thus, there were varying approaches to ageing among the informants. This has clear implications for the emotional experience and the reflections on how they have to mentally prepare for their ageing. The informants who thought they would experience normal ageing did not feel any anxiety or depression. Ageing was described as something that presented opportunities for development and fulfilment, and a chance to continue their disability policy commitment. However, those informants who saw ageing and disability as mutually reinforcing, and thought that ageing made the disability worse and vice versa, worried about later life. Frank, who had a more pessimistic view of ageing, also developed ideas about how to mentally prepare himself for his later life. It was important to find solutions to problems and to see the troubles that arose as challenges rather than obstacles. One should not focus on losses, but adapt and gather the necessary strength. Frank put it like this: "The need for mental work of adaptation and strength is significantly more for a disabled person who wishes to approach old age in a harmonious way."

A normal lifecourse?

The lifecourse in Western welfare societies can be said to be a kind of established social schedule (institutionalised lifecourse), based on biological/chronological age, but it is in fact about social age (Närvänen, 1994). A 'normal' lifecourse, with all that it entails, can also be said to be normative. The norms are concerned with the ability to get an education, a job, to support oneself, to function as a parent and to experience later life with quality, activities and good care. Such conditions of life as going to school, having one's own home, supporting oneself through work, raising a family and growing old with dignity should also be achieved at the right time in life. If this does not happen, it can be due to discrimination, lack of accessibility, prejudice, small or poorly allocated resources, institutionalisation (segregation), oppression or the like. To be outside the norm is to become different and probably socially categorised, for instance, as disabled. An important starting point for disabled people's experiences of ageing is the issue of gaining a *normal* lifecourse, including normal ageing.

Jönson and Taghizadeh Larsson (2006; 2009) problematise the various approaches to the normative lifecourse that is expressed in Swedish social policy, especially in disability and elderly politics. In later life politics the normal lifecourse divided into distinct phases is questioned, while in disability politics a normative lifecourse perspective is an obvious starting point (Jönson and Taghizadeh Larsson, 2006; 2009). Jönson and Taghizadeh Larsson (2006; 2009) note that there are ideological reasons behind these different approaches. The idea about a normal lifecourse is set against a relative idea of age. For disabled people a dissolution of the social schedule is not desirable; rather the opposite. This is because disabled people have not previously been able to live fully according to a socially established schedule, and therefore have lived their life outside biographical normality. The lifecourses of disabled people are often abnormal in one way or another.

Something that can characterise the lives of disabled people is so-called biographical disruptions, for instance, a traumatic injury. There are impairments that are static but others become more problematic with time, and for some disabilities, compensations are changing for the better, from a functional standpoint. Disability, then, is not a parameter that is static over time (Jeppsson Grassman, 2005). It is influenced by both improvements and deteriorations, on individual, technical, medical and societal levels.

Double discrimination

Another perspective on what ageing means for disabled people is the age discrimination that might occur with double discrimination as a consequence. The experience of being discriminated against because of disability is one that the informants shared and that constituted a strong motivation for involvement in the disability rights movement. A general impression that the informants had was that elderly people were also discriminated against. They felt that there was ageism in society, and therefore the risk was obvious that disabled people also encountered it (see also Andersson, 2008).

Eric and Oscar felt that they were discriminated against because of their age when they reached the age of 70. Frank said he had not been affected yet: "Maybe," he says, "ageism in my case is still mild, or maybe I have not developed the sensitivity yet." It was, he thought, worse for disabled people to leave work and retire than for non-disabled people, because work prevented the feeling of exclusion and discrimination.

When it came to the relationship between the categories of old and disabled, opinions differed fundamentally among the informants. The idea that these categories should not be mixed was set against a more pragmatic view that these groups sometimes had the same needs of availability. It can be argued that what is good for disabled people is also good for elderly people (Jönson and Taghizadeh Larsson, 2009). George did not think that in the case of disability, age should really matter. The problems were related to disability even in later life, and he thought that "the measures you put into the elderly politics area ... have perhaps some special features because people are 80 or 90 years old, but basically it is disability measures too." This attitude is characterised by an awareness of what ageism may involve, and does not set elderly and disabled people against each other.

In summary, I would interpret the informants' statements as follows: in strict contrast to the pragmatic view on mixing social categories stood the chronological/biological point of departure that insisted that disabled people's lifecourse should reflect the lifecourse of non-disabled people. This means that living conditions for the disabled in each section of life should be matched by the conditions of most others of the same chronological/biological age. The social schedule should be followed and deviations from the normal lifecourse should be considered as failures, and as consequences of discrimination.

A good life in later life

Despite experiences of discrimination and various problems with bodily functions and impairments, several of the informants of this very special group of disability activists highlighted that they had a good life, "almost too good", Eric said. The implication of this is that they were healthy and strong and well, despite problems due to disability. All the informants said they lived a good life, with family and friends, and their involvement in the disability rights movement was also a source of meaningful activities and social life. Even if one gets old and ages, there is no reason not to continue to be active and try to influence policy. The increased restrictions, which deteriorating physical abilities entail, should not become an obstacle.

Inevitably, experiences of aging amplify deeper dimensions of life and the meaning of life. The informants of this chapter thought a lot about various aspects of life and its purpose, and this might be related to their disability and their lifecourse. Disability experiences bring existential questions to a head. A disability requires existential choices and it is challenging in this regard: 'Why me?' the interviewed thought in their teens. 'What if I had not been disabled' they thought when they faced obstacles, for example, in their education or career choices. 'Damn disability', they think, facing practical problems in everyday life.

I also asked the very difficult question of whether the informants would rather have lived their lives without disability. The answer I got was that this was a question that could not be answered, but if pressed, all of them would say that they would rather have lived their lives without disability. To say anything else would be an idealisation. But at the same time, not one of them wanted to forsake the valuable experiences gained from a life lived with disabilities.

Discussion

The aim of this chapter was to use a *political lifecourse perspective* to improve understanding of the links between disability identity, participation in the disability rights movement, narratives of disability history and views of later life and ageing. The informants of this chapter constitute a special group of people with strong disability identities. These people have always been very active and outgoing and they still are, despite their age. Their lives are characterised by a strong commitment to the Swedish disability rights movement and they have been disability activists over a long period of time. The work within the disability movement and their own experience of disability was an important part of their identities, and so was their historical awareness. Experience of disability had had an impact on their views of ageing and later life, of ageism and discrimination. They would like to think that ageing and later life should not be any different for them and for other disabled people compared to non-disabled, but in some ways they were.

The historical perspective of disability policies and issues shows the importance of contextualising interviewees biographically. The different attitudes that are expressed can be related to the person's lifecourse. The interviews reflect both the individual's life with disability over time, and also the actual historical time and the collective narratives of disability history. The political life stories of the informants have an impact on their attitude to ageing, as well the experience of disability policy issues during the late 1900s. So there is reason to believe that the informants' ageing will be shaped by the past, and since they have always been very active, it is reasonable to believe that their later life will also be an active part of their life.

With 'normal ageing' social gerontologists usually mean healthy ageing, which is ageing that proceeds without any specific disease or disability. The concept of normal ageing could also mean the ageing that most people are undergoing (Biggs, 2001; Krekula, 2006). In this discussion I try to explore what characterises disabled people's approach to ageing. Do disabled people have a different view of ageing than non-disabled people, and if so, why? What prevents disabled people experiencing normal ageing in later life, and what makes it possible?

The initial question in the interviews was whether disabled people had a different view of ageing than non-disabled, and if so, why. The varied attitudes I found among the informants to ageing were not directly contradictory, but they were different, mainly in terms of where the emphasis lay. Some of them had a more idealistic approach, while others took a more pragmatic attitude. However, the strongest opinion was that it was more difficult for disabled people to age than for non-disabled people. There was a risk of double discrimination and of being stereotyped; And ageing had greater physical consequences compared to others, with more problems being added to the ones they already had.

The interviews show that the informants discussed ageing on the basis of their disability. They therefore had an approach to ageing that differed from most others, that is, from non-disabled people. Disability was such a major part of their identity, and life had been shaped for so long around it, that it was impossible not to think of it. Also, there was no reason not to, and the interview itself inspired such a discussion. By this I do not mean that perceptions of ageing were totally different from most others, but there were essential features that differed.

A number of different perceptions of ageing can be highlighted, described and discussed, based on the interviews. Fundamental to attitudes to ageing is if disability is seen as static or changing through the lifecourse. If disability is viewed as static it is discussed in a different way than if it is seen as a phenomenon of gradually occurring change and deterioration (Jeppsson Grassman, 2005). These attitudes are also greatly affected by whether the social situation as a disabled person has become easier or more problematic over the years.

On the one hand, this means that there are perceptions connected with positive attitudes, saying that: disabled people are prepared for normal ageing which leads to restrictions or loss of bodily functions; disabled people are better prepared for and accustomed to infirmity and sickness than most people; And disability and ageing is basically the same as for non-disabled people, provided that disabled people receive full compensation for reduced capabilities (for instance, personal assistance). Another standpoint is that disability living conditions and situations change dramatically for the worse due to more problems in addition to those already experienced, but this is viewed as a challenge to which one has to find new solutions. On the other hand, there is a more negative strand of attitudes in the interviews saying that disabled people's living conditions and situations change dramatically for the worse when more problems arise in later life in addition to those already perceived. This implies a worsened condition; disabled people suffer from double discrimination, both ageism and discrimination based on disability.

Of course, these experiences of and attitudes to ageing are also similar to those of non-disabled people, including, for example, frustration, reconciliation, acceptance, resistance and grief. This can be said to represent one of the main positions in social gerontological research (Krekula, 2006). But beyond this, the informants expressed reflections and experiences of ageing, based on their experience of living with disabilities.

One main consideration in this chapter is the obstacles that prevent disabled people from living through 'normal' ageing and what makes it possible. Due to disability policy ideology there should be no difference between the ageing of disabled and non-disabled people. This is based on the effort to gain right of access to the so-called 'normal' lifecourse (Jönson and Taghizadeh Larsson, 2006; 2009) and here, disability history provides an important background to the informants' approach.

A disability policy reform that was often mentioned in the statements among the interviewed was the legislation on services and personal assistance of 1993. These Acts were seen to have symbolised an ideological shift compared to previous legislation. This was something that many of the informants emphasised. The meaning of the laws, ideally speaking, was that the differences between disabled and non-disabled people should be eliminated. This would also affect later life, provided that disabled people were allowed to keep personal assistance even after the age of 65. Oscar argued for this in a strong way: "It shouldn't be any different," he said.

The different approaches were evident in the interviews and are well worth discussing, but it is also interesting to consider what was not mentioned. Ageing as a time of reflection and withdrawal was not prominent in the reflections. Krekula (2006) mentions three categories of perceptions of ageing: the individual's view of him or herself, the individual's views on others, and finally, attitudes in society. For the informants of this chapter my impression was that the overriding identification was made based on disability. Ageing was not the main identification related to these three categories. One argues from one's own and others' disabilities, and identity is based on this. Attitudes within society were significantly present in the interviews in the comparisons between ageism and disability discrimination, but the comparisons were based on disability. The informants were transferring experiences and effects of disability to the ageing phenomenon. This concerned discrimination, which several of the interviewed said they had experienced for a long time. They also had other comparable experiences, for instance, of losses of bodily functions, being dependent on others and having to fight for their rights.

Perspectives on and experiences of ageing are in a specific way coloured by personal, social and historical consciousness. It is important to mention that the special group of people, interviewed for this chapter, were born in the 1930s and 1940s, that is, during a period of growing disability policy and identity politics. They have all experienced disability over a long period of time and their involvement in the disability rights movement has affected their perceptions of life and ageing. The political lifecourse perspective can contribute to the understanding of disability identity, and a disability identity can be an important explanation of attitudes towards ageing and later life among disabled people.

References

Andersson, L. (2008) *Ålderism [Ageism]*, Lund: Studentlitteratur.

Andrews, M. (2007) *Shaping history: Narratives of political change*, Cambridge: Cambridge University Press.

Barnes, C. and Mercer, G. (2010) *Exploring disability: A sociological introduction* (2nd edn), Cambridge: Polity Press.

Biggs, S. (2001) 'Toward critical narrativity: Stories of aging in contemporary social policy', *Journal of Aging Studies*, vol 15, no 4, pp 303-16.

Campbell, J. and Oliver, M. (1996) *Disability politics: Understanding our past, changing our future*, London: Routledge.

Chamberlayne, P., Bornat, J. and Apitzsch, U. (eds) (2004) *Biographical methods and professional practice: An international perspective*, Bristol: The Policy Press.

Gullette, M.M. (2003) 'From life storytelling to age autobiography', *Journal of Aging Studies*, vol 17, pp 101-11.

HCK (Handikappförbundens Centralkommitté) [Disability Federation Central Committee] (1972) Ett samhälle *för* alla: Handikappolitiskt program [*A society for all: Disability policy program*], Stockholm: HCK.

HCK (1992) HCK – 50 år: Handikapprörelsen i samverkan – Då, nu och i framtiden [*HCK – 50 years: Disability movement working together – Then, now and in the future*], Stockholm: HCK.

Hockey, J.L. and James, A. (2003) *Social identities across the life course*, Basingstoke: Palgrave Macmillan.

Holme, L. (2000) 'Begrepp om handikapp: En essä om det miljörelativa handikappbegreppet' ['Concepts of disability: An essay on the environmental relative concept of disability'], in M. Tideman (eds) *Handikapp: Synsätt, principer, perspektiv* [*Handicap: Attitudes, principles, perspectives*], Lund: Studentlitteratur, pp 67-78.

Holme, L. (2008) 'Det borde inte vara någon skillnad: Förhållningssätt till åldrande i handikapphistorisk belysning' ['It shouldn't be any different: Attitudes to ageing in the light of disability history'], in E. Jeppsson Grassman (eds) *Att åldras med funktionshinder* [*Ageing with disability*], Lund: Studentlitteratur, pp 27-52.

Holme, L. and Olsson, I. (2001) 'Handikapphistorisk forskning. En översikt' ['Disability history research: An overview'], in R. Qvarsell and U. Torell (eds) *Humanistisk hälsoforskning. En forskningsöversikt* [*Humanistic health research: A research overview*], Lund: Studentlitteratur, pp 209-42.

Hugemark, A. and Roman, C. (2007) 'Diversity and division in the Swedish disability movement: Disability, gender, and social justice', *Scandinavian Journal of Disability Research*, vol 9, no 1, pp 26-45.

Jenkins, R. (2008) *Social identity*, London: Routledge.

Jeppsson Grassman, E. (2005) 'Tid, rum, kropp och livslopp: Nya perspektiv på funktionshinder' ['Time, space, body and life course: Disability from new perspectives'], in E. Jeppsson Grassman and L.-Ch. Hydén (eds) *Kropp, livslopp och åldrande: Några samhällsvetenskapliga perspektiv* [*Body, life course and ageing: Some social perspectives*], Lund: Studentlitteratur, pp 19-52.

Jönson, H. and Taghizadeh Larsson, A. (2006) 'Ideologibaserade livsloppskonstruktioner inom handikapp och äldrepolitik' ['Ideology-based life course constructions within the disability and old age politics'], *Socionomen*, 5, pp 18-31.

Jönson, H. and Taghizadeh Larsson, A. (2009) 'The exclusion of older people in disability activism and policies – a case of inadvertent ageism?' *Journal of Aging Studies*, vol 23, no 1, pp 69-77.

Krekula, C. (2006) *Kvinna i ålderskodad värld. Om äldre kvinnors förkroppsligade identitetsförhandlingar* [*Women in an age-coded world: On older women's embodied identity negotiations*], Uppsala: Uppsala University.

Lindberg, L. (2006) 'Handikappolitikens utveckling – från institutioner till sektorsansvar' ['Disability policy development – from institutions to sector responsibility'], in P. Brusén and A. Printz (eds) *Handikappolitiken i praktiken: Om den nationella handlingsplanen [Disability politics in practice: About the national action plan]*, Stockholm: Gothia, pp 19-36.

Nirje, B. (2003) *Normaliseringsprincipen [The normalisation principle]*, Lund: Studentlitteratur.

Närvänen, A.-L. (1994) *Temporalitet och social ordning. En tidssociologisk diskussion utifrån vårdpersonals uppfattningar om handlingsmöjligheter i arbetet [Temporality and social order. A time-sociological discussion by health professionals' perceptions of possibilities for action in work]*, Linköping Studies in Arts and Science, No 117, Linköping: Linköping University.

Närvänen, A.-L. (2009) 'Ålder, livslopp, åldersordning' ['Age, life course, age regime'], in H. Jönson (eds) *Åldrande, åldersordning, ålderism [Ageing, age regime, ageism]*, Linköping: National Institute for the Study of Ageing and Later Life, Linköping University, pp 18-29.

Priestley, M. (2003) *Disability: A life course approach*, Cambridge: Polity Press.

Shakespeare, T. (1993) 'Disabled people's self-organisation: a new social movement', *Disability, Handicap and Society*, vol 8, no 3, pp 249-64.

Shakespeare, T. (1996) 'Disability, identity and difference', in C. Barnes and G. Mercer (eds) *Exploring the divide: Illness and disability*, Leeds: Disability Press, pp 94-113.

Shakespeare, T. (2004) 'Social models of disability and other life strategies', *Scandinavian Journal of Disability Research*, vol 6, no 1, pp 8-21.

Shakespeare, T. (2006) *Disability rights and wrongs*, London: Routledge.

Sjöberg, M. (2010) *Bana väg: Välfärdspolitik och funktionshinder [Pioneering: Welfare policy and disability]*, Hedemora: Gidlund.

Symeonidou, S. (2009) 'The experience of disability activism through the development of the disability movement: how do disabled activists find their way in politics?', *Scandinavian Journal of Disability Research*, vol 11, no 1, pp 17-34.

FOUR

Is it possible to 'age successfully' with extensive physical impairments?

Annika Taghizadeh Larsson

Introduction

The question in the title of this chapter is the point of departure for the discussion here: is it possible to age actively and 'successfully' with extensive impairments?

Recent decades have witnessed the emergence of a perspective on ageing that has provided a sharp contrast to the negative loss and decline perspective that has dominated gerontology for many years (Minkler and Fadem, 2002). A common trait among scholars promoting this positive and active view is to present avoidance or absence of disease and impairment as prerequisites for enabling later life to become a period of engagement and self-fulfilment. For example, Laslett (1989) argues that even if the preconditions for self-realisation and pursuit of leisure activities, characteristic of the so-called 'third age', are often greatest when one has passed retirement age, retirement as such does not ensure active and positive ageing. What Laslett describes as crucial, on the other hand, is a person's health and functional state. Similarly, characterisations of active, 'successful' ageing have been closely related to the maintenance of high physical and cognitive functions (Minkler and Fadem, 2002). Laying out their model of successful ageing, Rowe and Kahn (1987, 1997, 1998) highlight three hierarchically ordered features as necessary preconditions for successful ageing: avoiding disease and disability, maintaining mental and physical functions and continuing engagement with life. Even the critical voices raised against the notion of 'successful ageing' seem to assume that impairments naturally and inevitably exclude older people from adopting an active lifestyle. This assumed exclusion is, in fact, the basis for their criticism. For example, Blaikie (1999), Öberg and Tornstam (2001) and Minkler and Holstein (2005) have, among others, argued that the ideal of the active pensioner is likely to reinforce the stigma surrounding diseases and impairments in older age and to contribute to the marginalisation of a large group of sick and disabled old-age pensioners. According to Cohen (2005), comparisons between seniors with impairments and 'successful agers' should, for this reason, be avoided altogether: 'Those and others who have been precluded from the formulas to successful aging by illness, trauma, or other cause of impairment, should not be contrasted to the *successful agers*, and even by implication characterised as failures'

(Cohen, 2005, p 111; original emphasis). To sum up, the active senior who is 'ageing successfully' is, in academic accounts, explicitly or implicitly, most often portrayed as non-disabled, an image reinforced by a complete lack of visible impairments or tools such as wheelchairs, walkers or sticks in advertising and in media presentations of the modern, recreationally active senior citizen.

However, does an active and engaged lifestyle in later life necessarily require a so-called good state of health and functioning? Or alternatively, could it be that, today, there are ways to live a self-realising life even for a senior with impairments who uses a wheelchair and/or needs help from others with such things as dressing and using the toilet? In other words, could it be that, under certain circumstances, it is actually possible to 'age successfully' even with extensive physical impairments? If so, what are the prerequisites – and obstacles – to a leisurely active later life with impairments? These are the overreaching, and to date largely unexplored, questions that this chapter will deal with, referring to the lifestyles and experiences of women and men who have grown up and are growing old with early onset impairments during an era of technological advances and developments in the area of disability policies. That is, this chapter focuses on individuals belonging to a category that is seldom, if ever, mentioned in gerontology or in the literature on the modern, active senior citizen.[1]

Empirical point of departure

Based on the voices of 'younger elderly disabled people', this chapter challenges and problematises writings in ageing studies that present avoidance or lack of impairments as prerequisites of active, 'successful' ageing. Examples are taken from a qualitative interview study with seniors with extensive early onset impairments, aged 65-72, who turned out to have an unexpected active lifestyle (Taghizadeh Larsson 2009).[2] Unlike many of the contributions to the debate on active and positive ageing, not only the challenges, but also the possibilities of 'ageing successfully' with impairments, are considered. The empirical examples that are presented will, additionally, clearly point to the relevance, and importance, of acknowledging lifecourse dynamics in academic and political discussions dealing with the meanings and consequences of impairments in later life (see Scheidt et al, 1999). As highlighted, the participants' situation today and how it is perceived is related not only to how earlier stages of life have unfolded, but also to the historical time and changing social context in which the individual lives her or his life (see also Chapters One and Two), and with policy changes and environmental accommodations.

The seven women and five men who were interviewed had lived with physical impairments for between 30 and 68 years. All were retired and were users of some form of mobility support (stick, walker or wheelchair) more or less all of the time; nine primarily used a wheelchair. The diagnoses reported were the following: polio, multiple sclerosis (MS), cerebral palsy, spinal injuries, stomach and intestinal diseases, and other more uncommon diagnoses. In the interviews, the participants were not asked to provide any detailed information about their financial situation, but in the light of their accounts and housing standard, their financial conditions appear to have been varied. One or two of the participants seemed to live in relatively modest circumstances, and several said that they were used to economising due to scarce resources. At the time of the interview, seven received personal assistance in accordance with the 1993 Act concerning Support and Servics for Persons with Functional Impairment, which means that they had been assessed as having major and lasting physical impairments, and that they required extensive support and services. However, concerning choice in activities and freedom of action to pursue these choices they were, due to personal assistance, probably in a more favourable situation than most – or all – participants described in previous works covering the subject of disabled people's experiences of ageing (Zarb and Oliver, 1993).

It is also important to stress that the fact that the majority of the participants had personal assistance meant they were not representative of all Swedes aged 65-72 who have physical impairments. In 2005, the year in which most of the interviews were conducted, there were only 1,539 individuals in Sweden, aged 65 or older, who received personal assistance according to the legislation on personal assistance (National Board of Health and Welfare, 2006; Swedish Social Insurance Agency, 2009a). That same year, 135,000 individuals, aged 65 or older, received home help services from the municipalities (National Board of Health and Welfare, 2007). The seven participants who had personal assistance belonged to the first cohort of Swedish citizens with the legal right to continue receiving assistance after 65 years of age. This right to retain assistance after 65 was introduced in 2001. However, the conditions were (and still are) such that personal assistance had to have been granted before the age of 65, and the amount of assistance accorded could not be increased after the 65th birthday of the person who had the entitlement.

In the following sections, similarities between the 12 participants' lifestyles, on the one hand, and the academic arguments proposed by Laslett (1989) and Rowe and Kahn (1998) on healthy, leisurely active, 'successful ageing', on the other hand, will be discussed, followed by a section highlighting the prerequisites and obstacles to an active lifestyle with physical impairments in later life. To provide an in-depth understanding of the phenomenon in question, some of the participants and their situation will be focused on and presented in some detail.

Leisurely active seniors with extensive physical impairments

The emergence of healthy older people – without impairments – spending many active, 'successful' years in the third age has been described as a new phenomenon arising from a combination of increased longevity, compulsory retirement and pension systems (Laslett, 1989). This idea, that societal changes have contributed to changed experiences of ageing among the growing group of vital and non-disabled seniors, is widespread among scholars in the field of ageing studies.

However, hardly any seem to have considered the possibility that changes such as technological advances and developments in the area of disability policies might also have transformed the meaning and consequences of impairments in later life in a positive way. That this might to some extent be the case did, however, become obvious when the seniors in question in the interviews described what they had been doing recently, and what they were planning to do in the near future, or when they were asked to talk about an ordinary week and a normal day. Then, the image of rather, or very, recreationally active, committed individuals emerged. The women and men described how they went to the theatre and concerts, were involved in artistic activities, took part in language studies, sports and gymnastics, and travelled both within and outside Sweden. Several were actively involved in their community through volunteer work and in various associations aimed at improving the living conditions of disabled people. Some were active in providing supervision for their personal assistants and in handling elements of the administration connected with their assistance. They appeared, in other words, and despite extensive physical impairments, as continually engaged in life in a way typical of the 'successfully ageing' senior citizen (see Rowe and Kahn, 1998).

The current lifestyle of the participants largely seemed to be a matter of devoting their free time to activities that they had been engaged in to some extent even earlier, when they were still on early retirement pension or were working. As Margareta (aged 66), who left work when she was in her fifties, put it: "Much of what I thought was kind of hobby stuff before, I pursue in a somewhat different way now." Some maintained that the activities that they were now engaged in were the kind that they probably would have devoted their careers to if the possibility had existed. Among those who expressed this was Inger (aged 67), who was diagnosed with polio as a child. Inger said that she had applied to and been accepted by an art college when she was a young woman. At that time, however, the educational institution was located on the fourth floor of a building without a lift, which made it impossible for her, as a wheelchair user, to begin her studies. Today Inger, with the support of her personal assistants, devotes a good portion of her time to artistic activities of various forms. Likewise, other participants expressed how developments in technical aids had created opportunities for them, despite increased impairment, to engage in sports in ways that were impossible when they were younger. Hence, the dimensions of self-fulfilment that are characteristic of the third age, according to Laslett (1989), may also be experienced by seniors with early onset impairments. In some cases, this experience seems associated with improved opportunities, which have developed during recent decades, for disabled people to pursue certain activities. Even if one's state of health and function deteriorates during the lifecourse, societal changes such as, for example, the Act on personal assistance may, over time, have improved other aspects of the individual's daily life. One out of several examples of the latter is the story of Ann-Marie.

Ann-Marie

Ann–Marie (aged 65) was diagnosed with MS at the age of 20 and had used a wheelchair since she was in her thirties. A few years after her 40th birthday she lost the ability to move her hands and arms due to thrombosis. For Ann-Marie, getting personal assistance at the age of 50 radically changed life for her and her late husband.[3] From only getting help with basic needs from the municipal home help service, the couple were now free to plan their days according to their own preferences: "We felt that we were very privileged, you know. Now, we were able to get out and stay out for a long time and decide what we wanted to do."

Today, Ann-Marie has personal assistance around the clock. She is an active member of an international art association. Through a monthly scholarship, a more established artist supports her in her artistic development for a few hours every Wednesday (Ann-Marie uses her mouth when she paints). Aside from being one of the participants engaged in artistic activities and gymnastics, Ann-Marie is also among those who, and largely thanks to the personal assistance, have recently had the opportunity to travel abroad, despite increased mobility impairments and additional needs. In recent years, she has visited Denmark, Majorca, the Canary Islands and Iceland, and is now looking forward to seeing more of Sweden. During the interview, Ann-Marie expressed her future travel plans:

> 'On the topic of travelling, I probably won't travel abroad anymore. I've had enough of that. Although, sometimes I think that I haven't discovered all of Iceland yet. I should go to the northern part too. But no, it probably won't happen. I'll keep myself to Sweden from now on. And you know what; recently I had this idea to adjust Lennart's car so that we can turn one of the seats and I can have a wheelchair in there. In that way we can go on shorter trips alone. So that's our small project right now.'

Lennart, the travel companion and personal assistant who is referred to in the interview extract above, has, for many years, assisted Ann-Marie with tasks of many kinds, from brushing away strands of hair from her face to personal hygiene, meals and dressing. However, it is Ann-Marie herself, through a specially designed computer, who administers the assistance and plans the assistants' schedules – as well as her own daily life.

Bertil

Another participant is Bertil (aged 70), who has been retired about as long as he has used a wheelchair, that is, since he was approximately 50 years old. Bertil was diagnosed with MS when he was 40, but he questions the accuracy of the diagnosis. A few years ago, he was also diagnosed with diabetes. Unlike Ann-Marie and Inger, Bertil does not have personal assistance. According to his own judgement, he is not currently in need of extensive support. He has a security alarm ("in case I fall or something, which happens sometimes") and daily telephone contact with the municipal home help service. In addition to this he has arranged service on a private basis to have a person come every two weeks to help him with cleaning and 'petty jobs'. The nature of the petty jobs depends on Bertil's current needs. Bertil's home is adapted for wheelchair use. For example, the sink can be lowered to a height that makes it possible to wash the dishes sitting down, and Bertil's bed is designed so that he can get in and out of it without help from another person. In his electric wheelchair, the Permobil, Bertil moves about indoors as well as outdoors. The height of the Permobil can be raised or lowered, which Bertil reports to be an advantage when he does his shopping and has to reach the higher shelves. Asked about the relationship between his 'felt age' and chronological age, Bertil answered:

> '[I feel] much younger than I actually am, because I have the advantage of having always been very active and have always wanted to do something. And that, I think, is something pretty good. To sit and stare at a wall is the worst thing that I can think of. I don't want to end up in any of those institutions. I've seen those places; They sit in their wheelchairs and sleep. What the hell are they waiting for? No, I want to be able to do things until I die and just collapse. And because of that I probably feel a bit younger. [Especially] after a trip like the one I did just now....'

Feeling relatively young

As indicated by the participants' stories quoted above, the interviews challenge earlier discussions about the third age and 'successful ageing' by conveying a picture of retired people with extensive physical impairments as adopting a leisurely active lifestyle. However, in addition to that, the interviews question the arguments that a so-called good health and functional state is a prerequisite of being able to 'feel young' or 'not old' (see Öberg and Tornstam, 2001; MacFarlane, 2004). In a quantitative survey study conducted by Öberg and Tornstam (2001), a vast majority of the 1,250 Swedish respondents, 20–85 years old, reported lower subjective ages than their chronological ages. In light of this result, most of the participants in the study appeared as statistically typical since they expressed a sense of 'feeling relatively young' when asked about their subjective age. Some referred to their active lifestyle as an explanation. Bertil was one of them. In the interview extract above, the trip that Bertil refers to is a cruise to Finland with former colleagues, which he had returned from the day before the interview. This trip was presented as an example of his active life. Bertil appeared to be an active person in general. During the interview, which took place in the spring, he said that he planned to go on a three-week sailing camp in another part of the country at the beginning of summer. He had been to the same camp for six summers in a row. He had begun sailing when he was a little over 60 years old as a less risky alternative to his former hobby, gliding. Bertil's future travel plans also included a trip to New York. Furthermore, he was engaged in gymnastics, and devoted his time to various computer activities. Besides writing his memoirs, he spent time "involved in the stock market" at his computer, although he emphasised that it was a matter of small-scale share speculation. He also regularly visited a computer centre for people aged 55 and over, where he expanded his knowledge of computers. To sum up, through his engaged and leisurely active lifestyle, Bertil appeared to be a rather typical 'successfully ageing third ager'. As previously indicated, he was not an exception among the participants.

According to Priestley (2006), the narratives of successful and active ageing adopted by older people and their pressure groups to assert and sustain more positive identities in later life 'are premised on a view of successful ageing that has no place for impairment and disability. Ageing with disability is implicitly defined as "unsuccessful" ageing, and adopting a positive identity of ageing means distancing oneself from a disabled identity as long as possible' (Priestley, 2006, p 88). In contrast, not only does Bertil appear as an active and 'youthful' senior citizen, he did not seem to have been forced to distance himself from a disabled identity in order to adopt a 'successfully ageing' identity either. In fact, he was an active member of two different disability associations. The sailing camp that he participated in was organised by one of these associations. Bertil was also involved in various collective efforts to improve the living conditions for disabled people in his hometown.

Prerequisites and obstacles

In the previous section, some prerequisites to the participants' lifestyles were touched on. The extent to which the women and men in question were engaged in recreational activities depended on, to varying degrees, such things as technical aids and support services which provide for more than just the satisfaction of basic needs.

Control over everyday life – with personal assistance

For those participants who had personal assistance, the support stood out as very important or even crucial for the achievement of the lifestyle they had. They talked about the Act on personal assistance as "the best thing that ever happened" to them, and "heaven-sent". When life with personal assistance was compared to life with previous forms of support and care, such as municipal home help services, the possibility of influencing the choice of assistants, flexibility and greater control over everyday life were among the benefits highlighted. Some expressed the view that assistance made it possible to "manage oneself", which could be seen as an indication that it is possible to be relatively dependent on other people, yet to perceive oneself as autonomous.

Environmental barriers

It was also clearly expressed in the interviews that the opportunities to live a leisurely active life with physical impairments in Sweden might still be improved by reducing remaining disabling environmental barriers. For those who did not own a car or did not have access to public transportation adapted to wheelchair users, the possibilities of participating in activities outside the home were dependent on how municipal transport service was organised, for instance, the number of trips they were entitled to per year. One participant who had a gastrointestinal illness reported difficulty in finding suitable toilets and getting a *disabled parking* permit. Those who used wheelchairs also recalled problems finding adapted toilets and reported limited access in some settings. One pointed to high kerbs as a risk that might make you "fall on your head" when crossing the street. Another participant described public transport as a "danger to one's life", and several mentioned difficulties finding suitable hotel accommodation. One participant said that she gave up flying after her electric wheelchair broke on two consecutive flights.

In the interview, Bertil showed in a tangible way that a leisurely active lifestyle with impairments in present-day Sweden might still include certain problems, pointing to three large bruises on his forehead and cheeks. During the cruise to Finland, Bertil had fallen over in the boat cabin. He was upset that the cruise company's definition of a disability-adapted cabin did not match his expectations at all. In particular, there was no security alarm in the cabin. Thus, Bertil had no choice but to lie on the cabin floor for several hours before receiving help to get back into the wheelchair. Bertil was also among the wheelchair users who spoke of stairways as barriers to involvement in recreational activities. Before Bertil moved to the town where he currently lives, he was a dedicated bridge player. Once settled in the new town, he telephoned around to various bridge clubs in order to continue his hobby, but realised in the end that he had to give it up because all the bridge clubs were either located upstairs, or in a basement room, one floor down. "Stairways should be removed!" Bertil exclaimed in the interview.

The participants also explained how their daily lives required time-consuming organisation and planning. Users of municipal transport services had to book their trips in advance, and wheelchair users prepared their visits to theatres and restaurants by telephoning beforehand to enquire if it was possible for them to enter the premises at all.

Impairments

Not all the conditions for a recreationally active lifestyle expressed during the interviews seemed to be social or environmental in the sense that they depended on external aspects such as accessibility and design of support and services. In some cases, it rather seemed to be the individual's body – her or his impairments – that constituted a barrier to engagement in certain activities – or in fact, in other respects, to fully engage in a self-realising, active lifestyle. For example, social interaction is implicit in the image of what it means to take part in recreational activities. An unspoken assumption is that an active senior citizen does not feel lonely. However, for Christer (aged 65), access to social interaction was not a self-evident part of his daily life.

Among the participants, Christer stood out as particularly recreationally active. Getting an interview with him was not easy. It was not that Christer was reluctant, but he was unsure whether it was possible to fit the interview in with his other activities. When we finally met, after a couple of rebookings, Christer said that he used to plan the coming week by going through the newspaper's entertainment and cultural supplement every Friday. He described himself as a frequent visitor to theatres and concerts, with a broad musical interest that included blues, jazz and classical music. He also volunteered as a kind of "entertainment and leisure consultant" (the interviewer's/author's expression) for an association for visually impaired people in which he was previously employed. Through his good knowledge of what was going on in town, he helped other members of the association to get involved in cultural events such as soup theatres and lunch concerts. Besides this, Christer was also a member of a variety of associations. Asked about which associations these were, Christer took out a thick bundle of membership cards from his wallet. The bundle included membership cards for music, disability and retirees' associations. He was not particularly interested in the ordinary activities of the disability and retirees' associations, he said, but participated when there was something happening that attracted him, such as parties or musical events.

However, during the interview it also became evident that Christer's daily life was darkened by the fact that he was on his way to losing the ability to communicate with other people entirely. Despite his active lifestyle, he was, as he put it, bound to "become a hermit". Due to an unusual illness, Christer's ability to see, move and talk had been gradually declining since childhood. At the time of the interview, he could only tell the difference between darkness and light, and needed a wheelchair and support from another person to move about. It was only through help from one of his personal assistants that the interviewer/ author could grasp Christer's answers to the questions posed.

Birgitta (aged 68), who used a walker outdoors, did not see her impairment as a barrier until her four children left home and both she and her husband were retired. Before that, it would have been difficult to engage in recreational activities anyway, even without impairments:

> 'When the children lived at home and everything – it had not been so
> easy then anyway. I don't think so. But then it's clear that nowadays
> we would have been able to do much more. There are just certain
> things that one can't do. Like my husband has been to the mountains
> and went hiking with some friends. That would have been great fun.
> Just going out into the woods and picking berries, to be able to go

out and do such things, or ride a bike – he bikes a lot too. Recently he went biking in Denmark. Those are the things one could have done. I would have been able to come with him. Those are the kinds of things one misses.'

One of the participants who was a wheelchair user said that riding a four-wheeled motorcycle in the mountains might nowadays be a possibility for those who cannot walk, "but it is not quite the same thing", as he put it.

Impairments may not only prevent engagement in some activities. The fact that the time left over for various activities may be limited due to one's health and functional state was also expressed during the interviews. To move, eat, shop, cook, dress and manage personal hygiene may take a relatively long time, which in turn limits the time left to engage in other activities. Paradoxically, to some of the participants this seemed to result in having to be particularly active. Or, as Bertil put it, "because everything is done so slowly I have to be really busy all the time to catch up."

Age limits

So far, all prerequisites – and barriers – to an engaged and leisurely active lifestyle with physical impairments commented on in this passage appear to be independent of age. For example, the organisation of special services, stairways as well as extra time needed for dressing and eating are likely to affect an individual's opportunities to engage in recreational activities irrespective of whether her or his age is 12, 40 or 70.

However, some of the participants expressed a concern about not being able to continue living in the same way. Their concern was related to the fact that in Sweden, people with extensive impairments lose some of their rights to special support as they get older. This, in turn, provides the basis for age differences in regard to the possibilities for living an active life with impairments. For example, and as mentioned earlier, personal assistance has to be granted before the age of 65, and those who have been accorded this support at younger ages have no legal right to increase the amount of assistance after their 65th birthday if, or rather when, their care needs increase. There are similar age-related restrictions on car allowances.

The age limits concerning personal assistance and car allowances did not seem to have had any concrete effect on the participants' lifestyles. This does not appear as particularly striking, since the vast majority had just, or had relatively recently, become retirement pensioners. However, some of those who had personal assistance expressed uncertainty about what would happen to their support in the future. For how long would they actually receive assistance? What would happen when they needed help for more hours than today? What would happen if they needed double staffing (two assistants) to a greater extent than today? Also, some of those who no longer drove a car reported that they had got rid of the car for economic reasons. One said that she would still have had the financial means to own a car if she had had the right to a car allowance. However, her impairment had not required the customisation of the car until she had passed the age of 65, and then it was too late.

Additionally, several of the participants spoke about a radically reduced income in connection with their 65th birthday. That is, there was a financial change – for the worse – linked to the transition from early retirement pension to retirement pension at the age of 65 that left these individuals with a lower income as seniors than they would have had if they had been able to work until 65. The latter may be explained by institutionalised age norms embedded into the Swedish welfare system that prescribe that it is normal and desirable that citizens do not retire before this age (Taghizadeh Larsson, 2009). Among the participants who felt this financial change were 65-year-olds Ann-Marie and Christer. At the time of the interview, Ann-Marie was in the middle of a process in which she was trying to sort out what might be correct and reasonable regarding the information concerning her future finances as a retirement pensioner that she had recently received: "It can't be the case that they leave you out to dry. There ought to be a subsistence level," she said. Inger explained how she initially thought that the low retirement pension could only be a mistake:

Interviewer: 'Is there anything else that has changed since you turned 65?'

Inger: 'My budget. Disastrous. It was a shock. And I, I must be incredibly stupid. I did not have a clue /.../ So, yes I was shocked. And I called … those who are in charge of this payment and calculation: "This is very wrong." "No, that's what you should have," he said. /.../ "And there is nothing to talk about" basically. All he said was "That is right." But that's not possible. I cannot reduce my income by half.'

Interviewer: 'Was that the case?'

Inger: 'Yes, it became catastrophically much lower.'

Interviewer: 'When you became a retirement pensioner?'

Inger: 'Yes exactly, exactly.'

Interviewer: 'And after a short working life.'

Inger: 'Yes exactly. /.../ All I could do was to think. And I was just so desperate, I thought now I have to sell the apartment here and move away. I thought that would be necessary for a couple of years. But now I have decided that the money I've saved, I shall use it all. Or rather, I will stay here as long as I can. And then I'll just have to wait and see. I may not live or I'll have to move, hell, anywhere. But I am going to stay here as long as the money lasts. I've made up my mind.'

Inger was not the only one to reflect on the possibility of moving to cheaper housing in order to manage on a retirement pension. That the pensioners' place of residence was specially adapted to their impairments made this decision complicated. Concerning recreational activities, the transition to being a retirement pensioner did not seem to involve any lifestyle changes at the time of the interview. For some of the participants, however, it is likely that the financial consequences of a relatively short working life would eventually lead to reduced opportunities to engage in certain types of activities. Apart from the fact that, in present-day Sweden, a relatively short working life results in a particularly low retirement pension (Swedish Social Insurance Agency, 2009b), living with impairments often includes specific costs (Zarb and Oliver, 1993). In other words, retirement tends to increase already existing economic inequalities (Calasanti and Slevin, 2001).

Conclusion

Does an active and engaged lifestyle in later life necessarily require a so-called good state of health and functioning? Or are there ways today to live a self-realising life even for a senior with impairments who uses a wheelchair and/or is dependent on others for help? These are the principal questions that this chapter has focused on. The previous sections have illuminated how individuals ageing with impairments are likely to face specific barriers to achieving their aspiration for a leisurely and self-fulfilling lifestyle. Among these are bodily and financial constraints, and buildings primarily designed for those able to walk. However, based on the participants' descriptions of their everyday lives, the chapter has also shown that it is reasonable to surmise that a senior with extensive impairments can achieve a fairly engaged, self-realising and recreational active lifestyle – *if the necessary environmental, financial and supportive conditions exist.* Unlike Laslett's and others' representations of an active and 'successful' senior citizen, the study conducted shows that some people live in countries that can provide a relatively high potential to live with extensive physical impairments, and at the same time take an active part in social life.

The chapter has also pointed to the relevance, and importance, of acknowledging lifecourse dynamics in academic and political discussions dealing with the meanings and consequences of impairments in later life. As has been shown, certain activities that are part of the individual's present daily life with impairments are particularly valued or experienced as self-fulfilling and may be related to her or his opportunities, or lack of opportunities, to pursue these activities at younger ages. That the prerequisites to pursue these activities have improved over the lifecourse may, in turn, have to do with general developments in welfare, technical improvements and a long line of reforms that include legislation on the adaptation of homes and the 1993 Act concerning Support and Service for Persons with Certain Functional Impairments. In this light, the dimensions of self-fulfilment that are often portrayed as part of the active, positive, 'successful' – and healthy – ageing stand out as being just as available to today's disabled seniors, who have grown up and are growing old with their impairments, as to their non-disabled peers. In the case of seniors with early onset impairments who, for example, were accorded personal assistance in their fifties after having lived their young adulthood as wholly dependent on home help service, family members or friends, in a society more poorly adapted to disabled people's needs than today's, it does even seem particularly likely that they will experience self-fulfilment in later life.

An important part of the developments that make the participants' lifestyles possible has been the disabled people's movement (Ekensteen, 2003; Peterson et al, 2006). Members of 'the collected disability movement' (Swedish Government Official Report, 1992:52) were, for example, represented in the government investigation (Swedish Government Official Reports, 1990:19; 1991:46; 1992:52) preceding the introduction of the system of personal assistance implemented in 1994. Scholars in the disability field have also been important actors in shaping Swedish disability policies, and researchers and policy makers have frequently taken a protagonist stance and stressed the importance of disabled people becoming equal citizens (Jönson and Taghizadeh Larsson, 2009). By focusing on aspects of the social or physical environment that prohibit disabled people from living their lives 'as others', emphasis in recent decades has shifted away from the 'imperfections' of the individual to broader society and to questions on how to make the environment accessible.

Still, in Sweden as in other countries, engagement in critical thinking on disability is quite rare in official discussions on ageing policies as well as in gerontology. Rather than focusing on environmental and societal failures to remove barriers, disability in ageing discourse is, even today, frequently viewed through the medical model lens. That is, ageing discourse continues to espouse a perspective that stresses the inabilities of people with impairments and tends to overlook the environmental and societal limitations that diminish the opportunities to participate in society and to enjoy life. On the other hand, in actions against disability discrimination and in disability studies, there are few references to older disabled people (Kennedy and Minkler, 1998; Priestley, 2003). Although developments in rights for disabled people have brought benefits to many, including people who have passed their 65th birthday, the progress has favoured young adults. Sweden is, in other words, not unique in that older people with extensive impairments do not have the same rights to special support as younger people with impairments (see Kennedy and Minkler, 1998; Putnam, 2002; Kane and Kane, 2005). As has been argued in an earlier article (Jönson and Taghizadeh Larsson, 2009), this 'ageism' can be understood partly as the result of a successful endeavour to separate disability and old age from a historical conflation and to provide disabled people of younger ages with the same rights as non-disabled citizens. In this struggle, what is just and equal has been defined in relation to what is considered a typical and normal lifestyle for non-disabled citizens of similar – non-old – ages: children, youth and young adults. Thus, to some extent, the exclusion of older people can be understood as the inadvertent result of a struggle against other forms of prejudice; That is, as a struggle against 'ableism'. The tendency to separate disability from ageing and older people in disability theory and policy can also be explained by the centrality of workforce participation in these areas. 'Crucial "non-wage-earning" populations – children, homemakers, and the elderly – are therefore acknowledged only in passing in most prominent critical analyses of disability policy, despite the fact that they make up the bulk of the disabled population, at least in industrial and post-industrial societies', as Kennedy and Minkler (1998, p 758) point out.

Just as it is easy to find explanations as to why later life and older disabled people have been neglected in the field of disability, the rather blinkered focus on health and function among scholars like Laslett (1989) – that is to say, anti-ageists striving for a redefinition of older people and of post-working life (Gilleard and Higgs, 2002) – is not hard to understand. Due to economic, medical and cultural advances, senior citizens in countries like Sweden today are, in general, more healthy and vital than earlier generations (Wiggins et al, 2004). Hence, the possibility to fight ageism and the 'inevitable decline' perspective that dominates so much of ageing research (Swindell, 1993) comes in handy. This fight is conducted through other research that aims to normalise older people and to provide more 'updated' and positive images of ageing and retirement on the basis of functional ability among seniors (Jönson, 2001; Jönson and Taghizadeh Larsson, 2009). Another side of this strategy, however, is that it reinforces a rather one-sided, individualised and personal tragedy view of disablement.

What is unique about the men and women in this chapter and about their stories and lifestyles is that they manage to do something that anti-ageists and disability activists have so far largely failed to do. That is, they provide 'updated' and positive images of older people *with impairments* and point to the necessity of creating a society adapted to people with and without impairments *of all ages*. In this way, they could be considered as pioneers. 'Successfully ageing' healthy older people spending many active years in the third age may appear as a new, modern trend (see Laslett, 1989). However, seniors with extensive impairments living fairly active lives supported by technical aids and personal assistance represent an even newer and more modern phenomenon.

Notes

[1] The chapter is partly based on Taghizadeh Larsson (2011).

[2] Twenty people aged 56-72 participated in the original study. This present chapter is based on the interviews with the 12 individuals who were on retirement pension at the time of the interview. It was those 12 participants' accounts that stood out as particularly striking

and interesting, due to the fact that many of the discussions on active, 'successful ageing' implicitly or explicitly focus on retirement pensioners (see, for example, Laslett, 1989).

[3] Ann-Marie's late husband also had additional needs and they both received assistance at the same time.

References

Blaikie, A. (1999) *Ageing and popular culture*, Cambridge: Cambridge University Press.

Calasanti, T. and Slevin, K.F. (2001) *Gender, social inequalities, and aging*, Lanham, MD: AltaMira Press.

Cohen, E.S. (2005) 'Disability', in E.B. Palmore, L. Branch and D.K. Harris (eds) *Encyclopedia of Ageism*, New York, London and Oxford: Haworth, pp 102-12.

Ekensteen, V. (2003) 'Från objekt till subjekt i sitt eget liv' ['From object to subject of one's own life'], in M. Tideman (ed) *Perspektiv på funktionshinder och handikapp* [*Perspectives on impairment and disability*], Stockholm: Johansson & Skyttmo Förlag, pp 105-18.

Gilleard, C. and Higgs, P. (2002) 'The third age: class, cohort or generation?', *Ageing & Society*, vol 22, pp 369-82.

Jönson, H. (2001) *Det moderna åldrandet: Pensionärsorganisationernas bilder av äldre 1941-1995* [*Modern ageing: Pensioners' organisations' images of the elderly 1941-1995*], Lund: Lund University.

Jönson, H. and Taghizadeh Larsson, A. (2009) 'The exclusion of older people in disability activism and policies – a case of inadvertent ageism?', *Journal of Aging Studies*, vol 23, no 1, pp 69-77.

Kane, R.L. and Kane, R.A. (2005) 'Ageism in healthcare and long-term care', *Generations*, vol 29, no 3, pp 49-54.

Kennedy, J. and Minkler, M. (1998) 'Disability theory and public policy: Implications for critical gerontology', *International Journal of Health Services*, vol 28, no 4, pp 757-76.

Laslett, P. (1989) *A fresh map of life. The emergence of the third age*, London: Weidenfeld & Nicolson.

MacFarlane, A. (2004) 'Disability and ageing', in J. Swain, S. French, C. Barnes and C. Thomas (eds) *Disabling barriers – Enabling environments*, London: Sage Publications, pp 189-94.

Minkler, M. and Fadem, P. (2002) '"Successful aging": A disability perspective', *Journal of Disability Policy Studies*, vol 12, pp 229-35.

Minkler, M. and Holstein, M. (2005) 'Successful aging', in E.B. Palmore, L. Branch and D.K. Harris (eds) *Encyclopedia of ageism*, New York, London and Oxford: Haworth, pp 306-9.

National Board of Health and Welfare (2006) *Funktionshindrade personer – Insatser enligt LSS år 2005* [*Disabled persons – Services specified by LSS year 2005*], Stockholm: Socialstyrelsen.

National Board of Health and Welfare (2007) *Vård och omsorg om äldre* [*Service and care for the elderly*], Stockholm: Socialstyrelsen.

Öberg, P. and Tornstam, L. (2001) 'Youthfulness and fitness. Identity ideals for all ages?', *Journal of Aging and Identity*, vol 6, no 1, pp 15-29.

Peterson, G., Ekensteen, W. and Rydén, O. (2006) *Funktionshinder och strategival. Om att hantera sig själv och sin omvärld* [*Disability and choice of strategy. About managing oneself and one's surroundings*], Lund: Studentlitteratur.

Priestley, M. (2003) *Disability: A life course approach*, Cambridge: Polity Press.

Priestley, M. (2006) 'Disability and old age: Or why it isn't all in the mind', in D. Goodley and R. Lawthom (eds) *Disability and psychology: Critical introductions and reflections*, Basingstoke: Palgrave Macmillan, pp 84-93.

Putnam, M. (2002) 'Linking aging theory and disability models: Increasing the potential to explore aging with physical impairment', *The Gerontologist*, vol 42, no 6, pp 799-806.

Rowe, J.W. and Kahn, R.L. (1987) 'Human aging: usual and successful', *Science*, vol 237, no 4811, pp 143-9.

Rowe, J.W. and Kahn, R.L. (1997) 'Successful ageing', *The Gerontologist*, vol 37, no 4, pp 433-40.

Rowe, J.W. and Kahn, R.L. (1998) *Successful aging*, New York: Pantheon Books.

Scheidt, R.J., Humphreys, D.R. and Yorgason, J.B. (1999) 'Successful aging: What's not to like', *Journal of Applied Gerontology*, vol 18, no 3, pp 277-82.

Swedish Government Official Report (1990:19) *Handikapp och välfärd? En lägesrapport* [*Handicap and welfare? A progress report*], Stockholm: Allmänna förlaget.

Swedish Government Official Report (1991:46) *Handikapp, välfärd, rättvisa* [*Handicap, welfare, justice*],, Stockholm: Allmänna förlaget.

Swedish Government Official Report (1992:52) *Ett samhälle för alla* [*A Society for All*], Handikapputredningens slutbetänkande, Stockholm: Fritzes förlag.

Swedish Social Insurance Agency (2009a) *Number of persons with granted assistance allowance for December 2005 distributed by age and group of persons*, Stockholm: Försäkringskassan.

Swedish Social Insurance Agency (2009b) *About pension*, Stockholm: Försäkringskassan.

Swindell, R. (1993) 'U3A (the University of the Third Age) in Australia: a model for successful ageing', *Ageing & Society*, vol 13, pp 245-66.

Taghizadeh Larsson, A. (2009) *Att åldras med funktionshinder. Betydelser av socialt och kronologiskt åldrande för människor som under lång tid levt med fysiska funktionsnedsättningar* [*Ageing with disability. On the meaning of social and chronological ageing for people who have lived with physical impairments over a long period of time*], Linköping: Linköping University.

Taghizadeh Larsson, A. (2011) 'On the possibilities of "ageing successfully" with extensive physical impairments', *Journal of Human Development, Disability, and Social Change*, vol 19, no 2, pp 127-40.

Wiggins, R.D., Higgs, P.F.D., Hyde, M. and Blane, D.B. (2004) 'Quality of life in the third age: key predictors of the CASP-19 measure', *Ageing & Society*, vol 24, pp 693-708.

Zarb, G. and Oliver, M. (1993) *Ageing with a disability: What do they expect after all these years?*, London: University of Greenwich.

FIVE

Being one's illness:
On mental disability and ageing

Per Bülow and Tommy Svensson

Introduction

To most people, growing old means changes in their social life, economy and health. Gerontological research is often framed by the idea of life conceptualised as a process involving 'normal' stages of childhood, schooling, professional career, family, and where old age is seen as a final stage. Ageing and old age, however, are not static or fixed concepts, but their contents vary over time. Some current changes can be related to the fact that the population, mainly in Western countries, is becoming older. In Sweden, life expectancy has increased by about six years for both men and women in the period between 1970 and 2004 (National Board of Health and Welfare, 2006). Increased longevity has also been accompanied by a generally improved health in the elderly. The notion of a 'third age' has become well established (see Chapter Four). This refers to the period after retirement in which people live an active and satisfactory life that is not limited by disease or disability. This period, it is sometimes suggested, may be extended further and further before the arrival of the so-called 'fourth age', when infirmities and disabilities can no longer be postponed.

People who live a life with early acquired and lifelong mental disabilities often have a lifecourse that does not easily fit into these assumptions of a life with normal stages. They often face particular difficulties, such as social stigma in various forms, and the elusive and invisible character of the disability.

The aim of this chapter is to describe and discuss experiences and interpretations of life and ageing by people with long-term mental illnesses and disabilities. The main part consists of a presentation of the results of a life story-oriented interview study with a small number of older people with experiences of mental disability. As a general context for the study, some ideological and discursive perspectives on old age are briefly outlined. By way of introduction, we provide a brief historical review of psychiatry. This is important in understanding the negative image that people with mental illnesses and disabilities face in our society, even today. Being a 'mental patient' is to hold a negatively valued social role that has deep historical roots. This negatively valued role is something that people ageing with mental disability have to deal with. The chapter also briefly presents some background information on the living conditions of people with mental illness and the process of deinstitutionalisation, that is, the substantial reorganisation of psychiatry that the Western world has undergone in recent decades. This reorganisation has, in some ways, radically changed the living conditions for people who previously lived their lives within the walls of a mental hospital.

Early history of psychiatry

People with mental illness are often associated with mental hospitals, and thus with social exclusion. For a long time, mental hospitals were the obvious and only places where treatment was provided. The history of the mental hospital is long, stretching back from the end of the 15th century. With few exceptions, the early hospitals were not treatment facilities, but rather settings that looked more like prisons or correction facilities. Those with mental ill health were incarcerated with other people who, for various reasons, could not support themselves, such as beggars, prostitutes, people suffering from epilepsy and thieves. Mental illness as a concept did not yet exist, and the rationale for intervention was not therapeutic, but to maintain social order and to prevent begging. It was not until the end of the 1700s that ideas about illness and treatment of 'the mad' appeared, and psychiatry was slowly subsumed under the medical model.

During the first half of the 1800s, the building of institutions, so-called 'asylums' that were designed for 'the mad', increased rapidly in Europe. However, an initial treatment optimism was relatively soon replaced by pessimism when the asylums were filled with poor people who could not be cured. The patients' incurability was frequently explained by the so-called degeneration theory that suggested that poor mental qualities were inherited in the family and that further deterioration would follow with each coming generation, inevitably leading to the family's downfall. Psychiatric patients were now seen as unhealthy and immoral individuals, and the professionals' task was to prevent the spreading of bad genes through detention and, later in the 1900s, through sterilisation. Treatment pessimism, the idea that mental illness is incurable, and a history of inhumane treatment methods are negative images that have followed psychiatry throughout its history. Psychiatry is still associated with these images, that negatively affect, in different ways, its patients as well as its staff.

Deinstitutionalisation

Up to the mid-1950s the policy to meet the needs of people with psychiatric distress was to offer a bed at a mental hospital. However, the merits of mental hospitals were called into question, and critics argued that psychiatry was mainly involved in supervision and social control, not in healthcare. Studies also showed that long stays in mental hospitals led to a destructive adaptation to an institutionalised way life (Goffman, 1961).

During the 1950s the trend with increasing numbers of patients in mental hospitals was broken. This change began in the US in 1956 (Norton, 1961). The number of beds fell and many mental hospitals were shut down. This process, referred to as 'deinstitutionalisation', carried through at a high speed in some countries, and with a time lag and at a slower pace in others. In Sweden, the process started late, with the last newly built mental hospital opening in 1964. Sweden had, along with Ireland, the largest number of inpatients in Europe, about five psychiatric beds per 1,000 population (Stefansson and Hansson, 2001). In 1973, there were 37,700 psychiatric beds. Thereafter, the number of hospital beds gradually decreased and was down to about 4,500 in 2010.

The process of deinstitutionalisation was slow and the hope of reducing inpatient care for patients with severe mental illness did not materialise. The Swedish Parliament decided to reform psychiatry from the ground, and transferred 15 per cent of the financial resources from the county-operated psychiatric services to local municipal governments. This reform, called the Mental Health Reform, came into force in 1995 and clarified the responsibilities of county-operated psychiatry and the municipality respectively. Psychiatry was to develop therapies and to treat severe mental illness while municipal social services would provide service and support in housing, employment and an active daily life. With the 1995 Mental Health Reform the term 'mentally disabled' became official, signifying persistent difficulties in everyday life activities that are a consequence of mental disorder.

Standard of living and living conditions for the mentally disabled as a group

One motive for the 1995 Mental Health Reform was the knowledge that the standard of living for the mentally disabled was well below average in Sweden. In addition, people with mental disability had a lower standard of living compared with groups with physical disabilities. In a nationwide survey, local governments examined how many people in Sweden were to be considered mentally disabled, what needs this group had and how these needs were met by support from social services (National Board of Health and Welfare, 1998). The total number of mentally disabled people over 18 years of age was estimated at between 40,000 and 46,000, which represented about 0.6 per cent of the Swedish population.

Loneliness was a reality for the majority of these people – 17 per cent were married or cohabiting compared with 58 per cent of the total population. Educational levels were well below the national average. Since several of the most serious mental illnesses start at a young age, this prevents many from carrying through to higher education. Low education and long periods of unemployment have a detrimental effect on the personal economy through life. In a study of the effects of the 1995 Mental Health Reform on work opportunities, it was found that only 3 per cent had been working in the open market and all, including those who had a job in the open market, received their subsistence through the social insurance system (Bülow et al, 2002).

People with mental disabilities have poorer health than the general population. In a large meta-study, researchers found that people diagnosed with schizophrenia were over-represented in all physical diagnoses, and that the average life expectancy was 25–30 years less than in the population as a whole (Adamsson, 2007). The causes of this are unclear, but many scholars consider a combination of suicide, unhealthy lifestyle and the side effects of treatment to be significant (Ösby et al, 2000). The so-called second-generation antipsychotics have also attracted attention recently because they cause side effects such as metabolic syndrome that increases the risk of diabetes and cardiovascular disease – in the 'normal' population 4 per cent have diabetes, compared to between 15 and 18 per cent among people with a diagnosis of schizophrenia and treated with antipsychotics (Nasrallah et al, 2006).

Discourses and ideologies of ageing and old age

Ageing and old age have been associated with various images, values, problems and possibilities throughout history (Minois, 1989; Johnson and Thane, 1998). Within social gerontology, theoretical traditions have had a major impact on research into the social and psychological aspects of ageing, but they have also contributed in the shaping of contemporary social and cultural notions of the meaning of growing old and life in old age. With some over-simplification, one could divide social gerontological theories of 'normal' ageing into two categories: passivity theories and activity theories. Among the first category is the so-called disengagement theory (Cumming and Henry, 1961) that played an important role for a long time. This suggested that normal ageing is associated with a loss of abilities and capacities, loss of social roles, diminished interaction with other people and a growing social isolation, that should, to some extent, be seen as 'natural' for the ageing person. Theories rooted in symbolic interactionism, on the other hand, have stressed the importance of maintaining a high level of activity in old age. The acquisition of new social roles to compensate for the ones lost in old age is then often viewed as necessary to maintain a positive self-image and self-evaluation.

On a more openly political or ideological level of discourse, clearly oppositional views of the meaning of growing old can be discerned. On the one hand, there is the 'decline ideology' of old age (Gullette, 2004), where growing old is depicted as a journey along a downward slope in the direction of disintegration, with problems, disabilities and vulnerabilities amassing along the way. Growing old is seen as something that irresistibly make people incompetent, asexual, unattractive and useless (Atchley, 1997). The term 'ageism' is often used to stress the stereotyping, discrimination and aggressive 'we and them' attitudes that accompany this ideology (Bytheway, 1995). On the other hand – and, to some extent, as a way of combating this ageist view – in recent years an 'ideology of successful ageing' has gained momentum. Growing old is depicted as something one can choose to turn into a success story. Staying active, developing new interests and relationships and maintaining positive self-esteem by combating the external signs of old age are strategies associated with this choice. Sometimes this comes close to a denial of old age (Hurd, 1999), or promoting an idea of living where time can be stopped or deceived (Katz, 2001). Some critical writers associate the third age ideal, based on consumption and individualism, with this 'successful ageing' ideology (Gilleard and Higgs, 2007). Since this ideology or discourse often tends to promote an idea of non-ageing or anti-ageing rather than a way of growing old, it has also been suggested that it actually risks strengthening ageist attitudes (Wilinska, 2012).

These perspectives on 'normal' or 'successful' ageing are relevant when it comes to describing and discussing the meaning of growing old with a mental disability since these will reasonably include a comparison with the meaning of 'normal' ageing. How does the ageing process of the severely mentally disabled differ from that of the 'normal'? In what respects will the presence of a lifelong mental disability make the experience of entrance into old age different? On the one hand, with an 'ideology of decline' perspective, one could hypothesise that entering into old age would make the mental disability play a less important role in one's life. It would, perhaps, be part of a more far-reaching complex of disabilities – physical, psychological and social ones – that one shares with other ageing people. The marginalisation and stigmatisation that have been part of life with a severe mental illness will now, perhaps, be a normal aspect of life as an old person that one has in common with other (non-mentally ill) old people. On the other hand, in the light of the discourse of old age as a success story one could imagine that the mental disability would be an extra burden to bear. The efforts to be active and attractive, to develop new roles and to 'succeed' with one's ageing (or non-ageing) would be more problematic and difficult for the mentally disabled than for other ageing people, and one's distance to those who 'succeed' would supposedly be greater. We return to these alternative and contrasting frames of reference in the final section of the chapter, and reflect on their significance for the interpretation of our results.

A life story approach to the meaning of growing old with a mental disability

The lifecourse perspective has, for some time, been acknowledged as a fruitful strategy in research on old age as well as research on the experiences of living with a disability. The strategy relies on the realisation that people's experiences and interpretations of their life here and now significantly depend on how they perceive and value the lives they have lived and how they construct meaning and coherence in their lifecourse as a whole. The adoption of a lifecourse approach is often tied to using some form of biographical method where the subjects of the study are invited to talk about the lives they have lived. In life story research, a distinction can be made between different ways to view the relationship between the life story ('the told life') on the one hand, and the life that the story is a story about ('the lived life') on the other (Mishler, 1995). Wallace (1994) writes of three different foci that collecting and analysing of life stories could have: a focus on objective data where the story is a tool for finding facts about events and circumstances in the lived lives of the informants; A focus on subjective data where the story is a source of information regarding the ways the informants have been experiencing and interpreting various life events; And a focus on social construction where the interest is directed towards the informants' ways of constructing and presenting an image of the lives they have lived. This could be expressed in terms of three different questions that can guide the researcher's use of a life story approach: 'What happened?' 'How did the informant (at that time) experience and interpret what happened?' Or 'How does the informant (here and now) want to present what happened?'

The strategy we adopt in this chapter comprises all three of those questions to some extent. That is, we acknowledge that life stories are constructions in the sense that they depend on the informant's intentions, her/his identity and self-image strategies and often very subjective selections and interpretations when it comes to important life events and circumstances. But we also assume that life stories in most cases provide reliable information on actual subjective experiences as well as on what really happened in the lives of the informants. The knowledge that could be gained from life stories in our view concerns the really lived life as well as the interpretations and constructions that are expressed by the way they are told.

Since a reflection on similarities and differences between growing old with a mental disability and 'normal' growing old is an important part of our approach, we draw on two sets of life story interview data for our presentation and discussion in this chapter. Most important is a collection of interviews – made especially for this study – with seven people with long experiences of living with a severe mental illness. These informants – five women and two men, aged between 60 and 76 – all had extensive experience of long periods of psychiatric care in mental hospitals as well as (in recent years) of more open forms of psychiatric care. They were initially asked to tell the story of their lives in an unrestricted way. Their life stories, which were open in that they could choose what to focus on and what themes to elaborate, were then complemented by some directed questions about their experiences, interpretations and evaluations of growing old. We also relied on information from previously collected interview material. Ten older people (who were all well past the retirement age) with no known experience of severe mental illness and no history of psychiatric care were asked to tell the story of their life and also to share experiences and interpretations of being old and needing care of various kinds. That study (the results of which were published in Swedish in Svensson, 2005) will be referred to as the ANL study (Ageing, Need for care and Lifecourse perspective).

Life in retrospect

People's life stories obviously differ in various ways. This holds for the form of the stories as well as their content. But there are often also common traits and similarities. This is partly due to the fact that life stories are guided by conventions in important respects. There are strong implicit rules concerning how a life story should be constructed in order to be a life story (or a story at all). However, form and content similarities are also expressions of the fact that people who live in a certain culture, in a certain society, and approximately during the same period of time also have many experiences in common and share a set a values, norms and ideals. These similarities are often further strengthened if the people in question have certain life experiences in common that bring them together in some specific group or category.

We start by describing and illustrating some basic observations from the life stories of the informants that display homogeneous traits, and show how these similarities within the informant group appear especially prominent when compared with the life stories of old people in the ANL study. Common to the stories in the ANL material was that the degree of engagement, enthusiasm and richness of detail was greater when the stories dealt with the early phases of life, such as childhood, family life and work. Descriptions of those parts of life were often characterised by a positive evaluation. Even if life and times had been hard, there was often a strong sense of joy and pride permeating the stories. In sharp contrast to this was how they spoke about the later phase of life that they now lived. The stories here were empty of emotional colouring, scarce of words and displayed indifference or desolation. The life stories of the mentally disabled informants clearly lacked such a pattern. Their retrospective reflections had very little of positive evaluation of the early stages of life, and they lacked the almost idyllic or idealised picturing of childhood and adolescence of the ANL informants. When childhood experiences were touched on this was done with a critical or problematising attitude, and memories of abuse or painful events were frequent:

> 'Our mother ... she beat us terribly when we were children. It was beastly really. I was beaten with a stick of wood when I was a child....
> We were never told why. There was no safety and no one to turn to.'

In some cases we got the impression that the views of childhood were strongly retrospectively influenced by the long-term illness experience of adult life. For instance, one woman showed a photograph of herself as a little child and suggested that the illness was already detectable in the child's face.

In a similar way, positive evaluations of their work and professional experiences were lacking. Several of the informants were employed in periods of their lives – some in very qualified occupations – but none expressed this as an important component of the story of their life that they wanted to convey.

In the ANL interviews it was striking how every life story could be subdivided into definite 'chapters' in a similar way. The lifecourse was described as a sequence with clearly separate phases: childhood, school, marriage and family, work life, retirement and present life as an old person. The move between phases often marked important changes in the lifecourse, and this 'chaptering' provided a structure to the narrative. In the stories of the mentally disabled informants this kind of 'chaptering' was vague or absent, and the structuring of the retrospective look on life was made in a different way. Life was divided into 'before' and 'after' almost entirely according to events related to the mental illness, such as when they became ill for the first time, when they were first admitted to mental hospital care or when this or that symptom (such as hearing voices or having suicidal thoughts) appeared or reappeared. The impression is that those experiences had such a strong impact that they turned the attention away from more common turning points and life phase shifts.

> 'I had just finished my occupational training…. Then I worked for six months or so, but then the voices in my head started. And this was absolutely terrifying.'

The clearly accentuated difference in the evaluation of life that was apparent in the ANL informants telling of their work life on the one hand, and their life in old age on the other, was also lacking in the informants' stories. Changes or lack of changes regarding illness experiences appeared to be of greater evaluative importance to them than changes from work life to retirement or from being middle-aged to being an old person.

Self-images and self-image transformations

In the ANL study the respondents' reflections and strategies, when it came to self-images and self-identity conceptions, were tied to the active phases of life. They emphasised their roles as parents and elaborated on their occupational and work life achievements. The period in life when 'you were somebody', when you had goals to achieve and functions to perform, was highlighted as important when it came to identity and self-esteem. Some of these ANL respondents maintained that "this is who I really am", even though old age and the decay that accompanies it made this hard to realise. Some others described their present condition in terms of a lack of identity. Growing old, in their stories, was described as passing from "being somebody" to "being nobody".

In the present study we found no corresponding effort to tie self-image to previous work or parental roles. Several of the mentally disabled informants had worked for periods of their lives, and most had some kind of occupational education. However, in their life stories, those circumstances did not appear to be of major significance. The times when they had worked and acted in a social context were vaguely described and were often peripheral to the main information of the stories. The same held for experiences of parenthood and bringing up of children. When those items were brought up or touched on they were mostly dealt with in a distanced and summarily way.

The dominant component of the self-image and self-understanding that can be extracted from the stories of these informants is the illness experience. The illness retrospectively appeared to colour or impregnate most aspects of their lives. Occupational experiences and family life seemed to be additions or complements to the illness experience rather than the other way around. Periods of somewhat improved mental health, when they could work or be a parent, were depicted as parentheses or temporary pauses in the long illness career:

> 'There were for the most part just temporary employments here and there. Then when I was about to get a permanent position I turned really bad. I think my schizophrenia was there already.... Then I was better for some time ... and then I made my first suicide attempt because I saw no other way out.'

A prominent characteristic of the life stories of the ANL interviewees was to strongly stress autonomy and self-determination, which they described as characterising their active years. To have been able to take care of themselves – even in times of troubles and difficulties – and not to have had to rely on help and support from others were kernel elements in the self-image that they wanted to project to the interviewer. The stories of the mentally disabled informants were in sharp contrast in this respect as well. Within the context of the long-term experiences of psychiatric and other care and support, self-determination and control over their own lives appeared to be impossible to adopt as central components of a positive self-image. But this also seemed to imply that entrance into old age, with the accompanying increased need of care and support, did not entail the difficulties with identity loss that troubled the 'normal' ageing people in the ANL study. The illness experience as such also appeared to overshadow other considerations. It was felt that you carried along the illness you had lived with for the major part of your life into the shrinking autonomy of old age, and the difference was hardly noticeable.

Attitudes to psychiatry and psychiatric care

The respondents in this study all had long-term experiences of psychiatric care. In the collected life story material, there were references to experiences of mental hospital care at every decade, from the 1950s to the 2010s. Stories, comments and reflections concerning contacts with psychiatric outpatient care from the 1980s onwards were also quite common. The interviewees told of treatment methods that ranged from insulin coma treatment and ECT (electroconvulsive therapy) to various antipsychotic medications and to different social techniques.

The stories often revealed an ambivalent attitude to psychiatric care and treatment. Although positive experiences with medication and with personal encounters with healthcare personnel were mentioned in the material, there were frequent references to times when the respondents had felt mistreated, neglected or abused. This most often concerned recollections from life in the mental hospital:

> 'I went voluntarily to psychiatric care. And I was committed because I had become strange. But in the hospital … I felt really bad…. All these others that were in a bad shape…. It was terrible to be locked up in a ward … I was given loads and loads of medicine … and no one there to talk to.'

None of the respondents described the reorganisation of psychiatric care that has taken place in recent decades (the so-called 'deinstitutionalisation' of psychiatry) as something that had changed the quality or quantity of the care and treatment they received in a substantial way. Psychiatry itself, they said, had not changed. Recurring periods of inpatient treatment still meant experiences of dehumanisation and hopelessness:

> 'It's still the same. You walk up and down the corridors and you get fed.'

The respondents were frequently dissatisfied with present-day psychiatric care when it came to information on their illness, its treatment and adverse drug reactions. Some did not know what their current diagnosis was. One woman was very dissatisfied to have recently discovered that she had the diagnosis of schizophrenia, since she considered that she was able to manage her life in a way that a person suffering from schizophrenia would be unable to.

They thought of the home-based social services they received as a municipal service directed to old people in general, rather than as something inherent to community-based psychiatric care.

Growing old with a mental disability

When it came to transition to life as a retiree, a comparison between the mentally disabled respondents and those in the ANL study displayed significant differences. To the non-mentally disabled interviewees, the shift from working life to life as a retired person was in most cases an emotion-laden event. To some, retirement came as a sort of liberation that they had longed for. They described how they felt that their bodies were worn down and that work, which had previously given meaning and context to life, had become a burden that was very difficult to bear. To another category of ANL respondents, retirement was perceived as a change that emptied their lives of positive content and substance. Accepting and adapting to life as a non-worker, they said, had been a slow and painful process, and some still found it hard to find some kind of satisfaction in life as a pensioner.

In the stories in the present study, there were very few parallels to those emotional look-backs. Becoming a retiree did not appear as a psychologically or socially important event. In most respects the transition did not entail any dramatic change at all, and life went on in the same way as before. As self-image and self-esteem had been tied to work life or occupational roles to a limited extent, the transition to life as a pensioner did not seem to imply any perceived alteration of a person's experienced social value. Several of the components, or lack of components, of everyday life as a retired person that the ANL interviewees felt that they had to struggle to cope with had, to the mentally disabled, been part of their lives since long before retirement. This went for a lack of social relations and contacts as well as for a lack of position or function in a societal context.

In a similar way, the respondents of the present study did not seem to have experienced the lowering of expectations concerning life content and life meaning that the old people in the ANL study recounted. Instead, they appeared to be resigned to the necessity of living a life with poorer quality, which may be an adaptation they had been forced to make long ago:

> 'It's no difference really. You know, the illness is the same and I do not think of how old I am. I have hoped all my life that I would get well and be able to work and all that but I do not hope anymore … and it will be no difference and old age, I cannot say what it does to me.'

Living a physically and socially limited life, having your daily living largely restricted within the walls of your home and taking one day at a time with not much further planning was something that the respondents did not relate to being old. They primarily saw these conditions of life as tied to their mental illness and the functional reductions that it entailed.

The descriptions of growing old in the life stories of the mentally disabled could be summarised by stating that the most important element in their lives – the mental illness they suffered from and lived with – did not change in any significant way when they became a pensioner or an old person. It was the same illness that they carried with them into old age as well as its implications and consequences. It was an illness that they knew well and had learned to live with; it had a 'time of its own' and this was not in any special way related to their nominal age.

Loneliness and social life in old age

It seems obvious that old age often implies increasing loneliness and social isolation. The majority of the ANL informants told of a current life situation that was very limited when it came to social contacts and social relationships. For several of them, contact with their children was important. Even though they felt that they did not get to see them as often as they would want to, thinking about them and taking an interest in their lives 'from a distance' was important. In the life stories in the present study, there were similarities as well as differences in this respect.

They told of a life that had been often characterised by loneliness. When it came to relationships with their own children, ambivalence was detectable. Some spoke of their sons and daughters as helpers and supporters in practical matters such as in contact with municipal authorities or transport to hospital. Some mentioned visits from children as positive breaks in the usual daily loneliness in a way that paralleled the descriptions in the ANL interviews. However, there was little indication of a strong interest in the present lives of their children. The distance to other people that they described as a consequence of their illness also seemed to characterise the relationships with their own children to some substantial degree. One of them expressed this as a strategy chosen out of consideration for the wellbeing of her daughter, to whom she seldom told the truth about her real mental condition:

> 'I have stopped telling her ... I would like to tell her how I am but then she would not feel OK so I just say that everything is as usual.'

In some other cases, the informants expressed a wish on their own part not to have too close a relationship to the children, since this would put demands on them that they did not feel they were up to. The illness periodically consumed so much of their energy that there was not enough left to keep a parent–child relationship alive:

> 'Seeing the children.... There must not be too much or too often. I can't take it. It becomes too messy and then I get in a bad shape.'

Over all, there was a two-way attitude to the experienced loneliness in the stories. In some ways, being alone was something painful, but also often something self-chosen. One woman talked about having such tremendous anxiety and panic when alone at a particular time that she screamed and screamed until the neighbours called the police to come and take her away. The same woman also talked about actively opting to be alone for long periods when any kind of social contact would be detrimental to her mental health.

Some stories revealed the implication to their social life of the stigmatisation and shame that they perceived as tightly connected to the mental illness. One respondent talked about refraining from partaking in a family reunion since she knew that her sense of 'being of another kind' would be too painful. Another respondent described a conflict with her own brother who suggested that one of them would have to leave town because he couldn't stand the social downgrading that came with people knowing that the two were related.

Several of the interviewees still tried to maintain some kind of social life in a weak sense. They routinely went to one or another daycare activity and spent hours there. One man lived according to a very exact time schedule every day, spending two hours at an activity centre, one hour drinking coffee at a specific cafe, and three hours doing another organised activity for the mentally disabled.

The way he talked about following activities with compulsory exactness on days when he was not too afflicted by his illness symptoms gave a strong impression of loneliness even though he met a great number of people.

When it came to loneliness and (lack of) social life, as reflected in the informants' stories, it appears that the mental illness created loneliness in several ways. It made contact and relationships with other people difficult by keeping them away from social contexts where relationships could grow and develop. The presence of illness permeated the relationships they actually had and made them often choose loneliness over social interaction. As the illness was always carried by the people, they felt alone with it even when they tried to establish some kind of social life.

Thoughts on the future

The life stories also contained reflections on the part of life that remained to be lived. Here there were somewhat more similarities to the ANL stories. In both cases, the respondents tended to express a rather short-term perspective of the future, and there were hardly any plans or visions of life a few years ahead. However, in the ANL study this lack of perspective on the future was most present in the oldest respondents, and could be interpreted as indicating a realistic acknowledgment of life coming to an end. In the present study, a lack of planning for the future was obvious even among those who were in the early stages of old age. This suggests that the motives or reasons for avoiding thinking of the future were, to some extent, different. It is one thing not to want to ponder on a future that is not there, and another to shut one's eyes to a future that seems to offer little but a prolongation of conditions that make life here and now hard and miserable.

In the reflections of the non-mentally disabled old people, they were worried about the prospect of becoming seriously ill or facing functional decline, which would consequently make them more dependent on healthcare and social support, or force them to live in an institutional setting. These worries were exclusively about physical illnesses or dysfunctions. The mentally disabled informants told of somewhat similar worries, but these were peripheral compared to their reflections on possible future alterations of their mental status and capabilities. The risk of being forced to longer periods of inpatient care or of having to accept new medication with more painful side effects made thinking about the future depressing and frightening for several of them:

> 'And this is how I feel ... I have not got the strength to try any new kind of medication because it is really hard for me when they get the idea to switch and give me something different.... I cannot think about myself in hospital for the rest of my life. This is unthinkable. I'd prefer to die at home but of course you do not decide these things for yourself.'

In one case the respondent entertained some thoughts on 'getting better' in the sense of becoming less mentally ill, but with no real belief in the reality of this possibility. Much more common was a hope for a positive development, tied to the wish for more effective medication. This was about a longing for effective symptom reduction and for medication with fewer side effects, but also sometimes indicated a dream of a life without drugs:

> 'I am not cured of course.... But it doesn't show. The medication makes it become latent in me all the time. But you have to live somehow too.... I wonder what would happen if I stopped taking the medication. I think sometimes that one day, I shall quit the medication and see what I become.... If only I dared to.'

Discussion

The aim of this chapter is to describe and discuss experiences and interpretations of growing old with mental illness and disabilities. Our study shows that the informants' life stories and their interpretations of the meaning of growing old differed from those of non-disabled old people in several ways. It is relevant to ask to what extent this result is also valid for mentally disabled older people in general. The respondent group was small, the data collection strategy was open and relatively unstructured, and the results are therefore not transferable to any population in a statistical sense. One could argue, however, that the experiences of the interviewees were not unique. Even if the respondents' interpretations and understanding of illness experiences, their encounters with psychiatric care and their perceptions of negative social attitudes to mental illness were subjective and personal, there is no reason to suppose that they deviated substantially from those of others with similar life and illness histories. It should also be stressed that the respondents did not belong to the category of mentally ill people with the most severe disabilities. There is some ground to suggest that people who have lived their lives within the realms of inpatient mental care to an even greater extent and at a greater distance from normal social life will also display more dissimilarities compared to non-disabled people when it comes to ageing and old age.

People with severe mental illnesses and disabilities have lives that differ in important respects from those of most other people. This goes for external circumstances such as personal economy, professional and work life conditions, and social life in general. But it also goes for life experiences, the subjective interpretations of those experiences and the ways of perceiving meaning and the significance of various experiences. During the long time when the severely mentally ill lived almost entirely inside mental hospitals, their lives were conditioned by the very special social and material contexts in those institutions. After the so-called deinstitutionalisation of psychiatric care, they are no longer forced to live in isolation in a strict physical sense. However, it can be claimed that mental illness as a social institution in a more sociological sense has not changed much. The basic notion of mental illness as a chronic and hopeless 'otherness' has a force of its own that influences the attitudes of the 'normal' toward the mentally ill as well as the latter's interpretations of themselves and their lives.

In the respondents' life stories, mental illness often appeared as the pivot on which almost everything else in life turned. Estroff's (1981) conception of 'being one's illness' rather than having an illness as a kind of burden to carry around is clearly enlightening in this context. An important question is to what extent their illness interpretation and their way of making illness the most important component in life were due to experiences from interactions with 'the normal', with societal and institutional agents and with psychiatric professionals. There were elements of some life stories that strongly suggested that interpretations of the illness and its consequences were not based on personal considerations, but could be related to the articulated views of important others, such as agents of psychiatric care and treatment.

However, the focus of our discussion here is on the importance of the interpretations of life with a mental disability to the experience of growing old that the respondents actually made, regardless of how they had been shaped or constructed. One way to approach an understanding of the very clear differences between these interpretations and those of the non-disabled informants is to adopt a role-theoretical frame of reference (Turner, 1991). A reasonable understanding of the strongly positive value attached to work life and parental life by the ANL respondents is that this stemmed from the experience of having been incumbents of socially and culturally positively valued roles. Those old people put forward as a kernel element of their retrospective interpretation of their life that they had met the demands that could be directed to an adult member of their culture and society. For several of them, those roles were also extremely important in a retrospective evaluation of their lifecourse as well as in a statement of an identity and a self-image that they were also now eager to project in life as an old person. This focus on conventionally positively sanctioned roles was almost completely absent in the life stories and reflections of the mentally disabled informants. This did not seem to be due to an absence of such roles in their lives. Our impression was rather that these roles and their importance were overshadowed by another ascribed role: the role of the mentally ill. This appeared to dominate the description of their relationships to others and to society and the image of themselves and of whom they had been and still were. It could perhaps be expected that the socially accepted roles the respondents had had should be used as counterweights to the stigmatised role as mentally ill. They could then have worked as an argument for a claim of 'a true self', somewhat like some of the old people in the ANL study claimed an occupational or parental identity behind the forced role as an old person. But if you 'are' your illness, this does not seem to work. The role as mentally ill seems to be so strongly internalised and taken for granted that distancing from it is impossible.

The notion of role transitions is also relevant in this context. Society or culture supplies a number of expected turning points when a person leaves a certain role and enters another, such as leaving childhood and adolescence and entering adulthood, or leaving single life and becoming a married man or woman to start a family. In retrospective life stories such role transitions often function as markers of significant changes of direction and content of the lifecourse. The importance of role transitions in this sense was strongly indicated in the life stories of the ANL respondents. Above all, three such changes were stressed: becoming a grown-up and entering work life, having children, and retiring from work. In the present study, one single role transition was stressed as decisive to the structure of the life story: the transition from being mentally healthy or 'normal' to being mentally ill. It also appeared to be irreversible, according to the interpretation of the informants. There was, so to speak, no role transition that took you out of the role of the mentally ill.

Let us finally return to the diverging ideological and discursive frames of reference for understanding the psychological and social aspects of growing old. Could the 'decline ideology' of old age or 'the ideology of successful ageing' be applied in a fruitful way to the life stories of the mentally disabled respondents? It appears that these frames of reference presuppose lifecourses and life stories that do not include severe mental dysfunctions and disabilities. These take for granted that growing old entails, or implies a risk of, substantial changes when it comes to psychological and social conditions and circumstances. Old age is supposed to involve a loss, or a threat, of diminished life opportunities and qualities of the well-functioning 'normal' person, that must either be accepted or combated. In the life stories of the interviewees, expressions of such a qualitative change were largely missing. The suggested frames of reference therefore seem irrelevant. There is not much in the stories that indicates a growing passivity when it comes to social contacts and relationships or a lowered level of activities as a consequence of entering old age. This is, of course, due to the fact that the informants were used to an isolated and introverted life, penetrated by the illness experience. Much of the anticipated misery that characterises the everyday life of the old person according to 'the decline ideology' was well known to these respondents for a larger part of their lives. When it comes to the 'ideology of successful ageing' and its visions of staying productive and attractive long after retirement, it appears that having lived a life with a severe mental disability implies having accepted the absence of those qualities. It seems reasonable to suggest that, to a large extent, talk of a third age excludes people with severe and lifelong mental illnesses and disabilities. In several important respects, the life stories of the informants articulate a picture of a life where many of the characteristics of the fourth age arrive long before the third age is supposed to start.

References

Adamsson, U. (2007) 'Metabolic effects of antipsychotic medications', Presentation at the Swedish Association for Diabetology, 9 May, Danderyd Hospital, Stockholm.

Atchley, R.C. (1997) *Social forces and ageing: An introduction to social gerontology*, Belmont, CA: Wadsworth.

Bülow, P., Svensson, T. and Hansson, J.-H. (2002) 'Long-term consequences of the reformation of psychiatric care: A 15-year follow-up study', *Nordic Journal of Psychiatry*, vol 56, no 2, pp 15–21.

Cumming, E. and Henry, W.E. (1961) *Growing old*, New York: Basic Books.

Estroff, S. (1981) *Making it crazy: An ethnography of psychiatric clients in an American community*, Berkeley, CA: University of California Press.

Gilleard, C. and Higgs, P. (2007) 'The third age and the baby-boomers. Two approaches to the structuring of later life', *International Journal of Ageing and Later Life*, vol 2, no 2, pp 13–30.

Goffman, E. (1961) *Asylums: Essays on the social situation of mental patients and other inmates*, New York: Anchor Books.

Gullette, M.M. (2004) *Aged by culture*, Chicago, IL: University of Chicago Press.

Hurd, L.C. (1999) '"We are not old!": older women's negotiation aging and oldness', *Journal of Aging Studies*, vol 13, no 4, pp 419–39.

Johnson, P. and Thane, P. (1998) *Old age from antiquity to post-modernity*, London: Routledge.

Katz, S. (2001) 'Growing older without ageing? Positive ageing, anti-ageism, and anti-ageing', *Generations*, vol 25, no 4, pp 27–32.

Minois, G. (1989) *History of old age: From antiquity to renaissance*, Chicago, IL: University of Chicago Press.

Mishler, E.G. (1995) 'Models of narrative analysis: A typology', *Journal of Narrative and Life History*, vol 5, no 2, pp 87–123.

Nasrallah, H.A., Meyer, J., Goff, D., McEvoy, J., Davis, S., Stroup, T. and Lieberman, J. (2006) 'Low rates of treatment for hypertension, dyslipidemia and diabetes in schizophrenia: data from the CATIE schizophrenia trial sample at baseline', *Schizophrenia Research*, vol 86, no 1–3, pp 15–22.

National Board of Health and Welfare (1998) *Reformens första tusen dagar. Årsrapport för psykiatrireformen 1998* [*The reform's first thousand days. Annual report in 1998 of the mental health reform*], Stockholm: National Board of Health and Welfare.

National Board of Health and Welfare (2006) *Social rapport* [*Social report*], Stockholm: National Board of Health and Welfare.

Norton, A. (1961) 'Mental hospital ins and outs: a survey of patients admitted to a mental hospital in the past 30 years', *British Medical Journal*, vol 25, pp 528–36.

Östby, U., Correia, N., Brandt, L., Ekbom, A. and Sparen, P. (2000) 'Mortality and causes of death in schizophrenia in Stockholm County, Sweden', *Schizophrenia Research*, vol 45, no 1–2, pp 21–8.

Stefansson, C.-G. and Hansson, L. (2001) 'Mental health care reform in Sweden, 1995', *Acta Psychiatrica Scandinavica*, vol 104, supplement 410, pp 82–8.

Svensson, T. (2005) 'Ålderdom, omsorgsberoende och livsperspektiv' ['Ageing, need for care, and life course perspective'], in I. Nordin, P.-E. Liss and T. Svensson (eds) *Målsättningar och verklighet – Vård och omsorg i kommunal regi* [*Objectives and realities – Municipal care and caring*], Rapport 2005:5, Centrum för kommunstrategiska studier, Linköping University, pp 59-119.

Turner, J.H. (1991) 'Structural role theory', in J.H. Turner (ed) *The structure of sociological theory*, Belmont, CA: Wadsworth, pp 410-24.

Wallace, J.B. (1994) 'Life stories', in J.F.G. Gubrium and A. Sankar (eds) *Qualitative methods in ageing research*, London: Sage Publications, pp 137-54.

Wilinska, M. (2012) *Spaces of (non)ageing. A discursive study of inequalities we live by*, Dissertation series No 24, Jönköping: School of Health Sciences, Jönköping University.

SIX

In the shade of disability reforms and policy: Parenthood, ageing and lifelong care

Anna Whitaker

'We are a disabled family!'

Introduction

This short but concise quote captures one of this chapter's key assumptions: that the experience of ageing with a lifelong disability is something that not only influences the disabled individual, but also very much contributes to shaping the lives of the family members (DeMarle and le Roux, 2001; Dowling and Dolan, 2001; Brett, 2002; Shakespeare, 2006). While the other chapters of this book build on stories of ageing disabled people, this chapter focuses on ageing parents and their personal experiences of having closely followed a disabled child growing up and becoming adult, and also considers in what ways this experience has shaped their lives – in an historical era marked by many changes and reforms in policies regarding disability.

The aim of this chapter is to describe and analyse aged parents' experiences of having followed a child with disability throughout the lifecourse, and of providing help and care for this child, including in later life. Various events and circumstances that have contributed to shaping the parents' lifecourse are described. The main questions are: what does the parents' caring role entail over time? How do parents view their own lifecourse in relation to this experience? What impacts have changed ideologies and policies had on their lives? What are the implications of ageing and becoming old to the parents? To date, these questions have only been studied to a limited extent.

This chapter is based on a qualitative study carried out during 2006 and 2007 in Sweden. Biographical in-depth interviews were conducted with 16 family members – parents and siblings – close to people with various disabilities (mainly physical) who were born between 1957 and 1982. The focus here, however, is on the 12 *parents*, nine women and three men. The parents were in the age range of 52 to 85 (ten were over the age of 65 and living as pensioners), and their adult disabled children were aged between 25 and 50. The children of the interviewed parents had different kinds of impairments, the most common being cerebral palsy and spina bifida. Four of the adult children had more uncommon diseases/syndromes, and the vast majority were born with the impairment. The characteristics and symptoms of the impairment were factors that were sometimes significant to the parents' experiences described in this chapter, but the particular impairments were *not* the criteria for the sample, nor did they form the basis for analysis or conclusions. The sampling criteria were based, instead, on the rationale that these parents could look back on the experience of having closely followed the growing up and transition to adulthood of the disabled child.

A predominant theme in this chapter deals with the parents' *caring role and responsibility* for the child, also as an adult and after leaving the parents' home. Today, the international literature on informal help and family care, in its broad sense, is extensive (see, for example, Gubrium, 1995; Hansson et al, 2000; Sand, 2005; Lamura et al, 2008; Eurofamcare, 2009). This huge body of research, however, is primarily concerned with informal/family care *to older people*, while knowledge about informal/family care to younger adults (younger than 65) with particular care needs – the long-term ill or disabled people – is, on the contrary, quite limited (Jeppsson Grassman et al, 2009). An explanation for this could be that this group of caregivers is relatively small. Yet surveys carried out in Sweden over the past 20 years (Statistics Sweden, 1992; Swedish Government Official Report, 2001:56; Swedish Research Institute for Disability Policy, 2005) point to the fact that help and care from family members is extensive among disabled people aged between 16 and 64. Other Swedish surveys indicate that informal care to those with long-term illness or disability (aged 18-64) is quite common, that informal carers provide many hours of unpaid work every month, and that they are likely to be more vulnerable than the population in general (Jeppsson Grassman et al, 2009; See also Olsson et al, 2005). Research on family/informal care in the disability field is dominated by studies about caregiving to *young* disabled children and their families, on the one hand (see, for example, Read, 2000; Brett, 2002; Todd and Jones, 2005), and informal care to *intellectually* disabled people, on the other hand, with a growing interest in the ageing process of these people and its consequences for parents and siblings (see, for example, Dew et al, 2004; Jokinen and Brown, 2005; McConkey, 2005). However, some earlier articles have shed light on the invisible work and the challenges that ageing parents of disabled adults might face (Jennings, 1987; Greenberg et al, 1993), and revealed that parents bear the brunt of caregiving (Hallum and Krumbolz, 1993; Ray, 2002).

Family care and disability – incompatible concepts?

Another reason for the limited interest in these issues could be the fact that the concept of 'care' has been considered to imply a subordination of the care recipient to the caregiver (Morris, 1993). The same goes for the concept of 'family care' in relation to disabled adults (Borsay, 1990; Jeppsson Grassman et al, 2009). The care concept has been the subject of massive criticism, not least from the disability movement (Shakespeare, 2006), and within (Swedish) disability policy it is associated with an ambiguousness that is partly related to the explicit goal of changing attitudes towards people with disabilities 'from objects for care to participating citizens' (Government Bill 1999/2000:79). The basis for this can be found in the disability movement and its struggle for better living conditions and social status for disabled people. An explicit goal has been to bring about a shift of power from the caregiver to the disabled person (Keith, 1992; Morris, 1997; Glucksmann, 2006). The right to personal assistance has been crucial in this struggle. In the light of this the care concept has not only become politically incorrect but is also ideologically associated with negative factors such as dependence, powerlessness and subordination. Thus, there are understandable reasons for why parts of the disability movement are critical towards the care concept, but this is quite problematic if these constitute a motive for why the experiences of caregiving among families have not been acknowledged within *research*.

In recent years, however, researchers have called for and initiated a more nuanced discussion of the role of family – and perhaps in particular the role of parents – in disabled people's lives (Avery, 1999; Shakespeare, 2006). Studies have shown that parents develop an ability to see the child's living conditions from the child's own perspective – an 'inside perspective' (Gustavsson, 1998, p 139) or a 'minority view', and in accordance with that, they *act in alliance* with their disabled child against oppression and exclusion (Dowling and Dolan, 2001; Brett, 2002), even after the child has grown into an adult (Bjarnason, 2002).

Parenthood, care and disability from a lifecourse perspective

The parents' accounts of having closely followed the disabled child growing up and becoming adult are also accounts of a specific historical time. As previously described in Chapter One, the *historical era* and *location* that is of interest in this book is the period of welfare reforms, not least disability policy reforms, from the early 1960s and onward, in Sweden. Theories of normalisation were developed early (Nirje, 1980), and the ideas of social integration and normalisation that are relevant to this chapter meant that children should no longer be institutionalised, but instead should stay with and grow up in their families under as normal conditions as possible. Of course, this ideological turn was particularly important to several of the interviewed parents. Some belonged to what has been called the 'first generation of integration' (Gustavsson, 1998, p 34). During this time a rapid phasing out of institutions and care homes could be seen in Sweden. This was a time of significant transition when it comes to school, housing and social services in general to people with disabilities and families with disabled children (McElwee, 2000). Care allowances, technical aids, extended childcare, school reforms, coordinated rehabilitation and respite care were other important reforms during the 1960s, 1970s and 1980s, all of which have facilitated the families' everyday lives in various ways. But of all the disability reforms during the last few decades, none has been described as being of such significance to parents and their children as the 1993 Act concerning Support and Service for Persons with Certain Functional Impairments, which came into force in 1994 and marked a great change in the parents' and their children's lives. Since the parents in this study belonged to different cohorts – some were born in the 1920s, others in the mid-1950s – and their children were born during different decades, between 1957 and 1982, all these disability reforms and social changes have had different impacts at different points of time in their lives as families and as individuals.

In the interviews with parents, an aim was to identify if and in what way social changes and reforms had contributed to shaping their lives over time (Alwin, 1995; Giele and Elder, 1998). During the interviews, the parents were therefore given the opportunity to relate their personal experiences and stories to specific social changes and reforms, especially in the disability field, at particular historical moments, and to reflect on what this had meant to them and to their lives. This methodological strategy facilitated the identification of conditions that they perceived to have contributed to shaping their lifecourse.

Time as an analytic theme has also given structure to the chapter. It begins with the parents 'looking back' on central events linked to the experience of having a child with disabilities. This is followed by a section describing their care responsibility and in what way it is manifested *today*. The focus of the third section is on what impact these experiences had on the parents' lives. Finally a section follows on the parents' thoughts about the future – including their feelings about ageing and death. The chapter is rounded off with a concluding discussion.

Looking back

The interviewed parents' biographies entail important life transitions related to the experience of having a child with disabilities, revealing their care responsibility in different life phases. To grasp the impact this has had on parents' lives *over time*, it is necessary to consider earlier events. In this first section, three important events are focused on: (1) the moment of the discovery of the child's disability, and the following early years; (2) the child's transition to adulthood; And (3) the assistance reform in 1993/94.

When everything changed – having a child with disability

A salient and emotion-laden theme in the parents' biographies was the moment when it was discovered that their child had a disabling impairment. This event, which often coincided with the birth of the child, truly represents a biographical disruption in the parents' lives (Bury, 1982; Jarkman, 1996). Within a few moments of upheaval, their expectations and hopes for the child and of becoming a family were completely overthrown. Some had obvious difficulty talking about this even though it had happened 30, 40 and in some cases even more than 50 years previously. The strong emotions were partly linked to the shock on receiving the information that their child was impaired ("I just cried, and cried, and cried, I cried constantly for three weeks"), it was partly linked to the disappointment and anger over the reactions, behaviour and prejudices of professionals ("the doctor said 'leave the child at an institution and go home and make a new child'") and sometimes also of relatives and friends. Regardless of whether this happened at the end of the 1950s or in the early 1980s, the parents described receiving relatively poor support from the professionals, and this result corresponds with earlier studies (Jarkman, 1996; Dowling and Dolan, 2001; Bjarnason, 2002).

These experiences were often expressed as what have been labelled 'tragic stories' (Avery, 1999), but the parents clearly underlined their right to these stories, the forbidden thoughts and the forbidden grief (Fyhr, 2002). *But* – and this cannot be emphasised enough – the drama and grief that this experience was often associated with, and the disruption it caused in the parents' lives, did *not* diminish the love, joy and pride the parents expressed about having a child who had survived and had grown up and reached a high age against all the odds. Neither did it stand in opposition to the fact that over the years the parents had developed a 'minority group perspective' and had often acted – and still act – in alliance with their adult child against oppression and exclusion.

All of the interviewed parents – including those whose children were born in the late 1950s when institutionalisation was expected – kept their children at home and took care of them, sometimes with some minor support from the public health and care sector. This is an example of the disability policy of de-institutionalisation and normalisation that gradually gained new ground in the early 1960s in Sweden. A consequence of this was a heavy care responsibility for the families. The parents' retrospectives revealed that they provided comprehensive care for the child during the upbringing. In their stories, when describing these early years, the parents often referred to the "evening work", "night-work" and the like, which meant various types of activities considered to involve a kind of care that went beyond ordinary responsibility as parents, illuminating a form of parental work that is seldom made visible in research (Ray, 2002). This is a matter of helping the child with all kinds of practical activities in daily life, as well as physical care such as help with food and eating, getting dressed and undressed, help with bathing and going to the toilet ("He needed help with everything, just everything"). It could be about giving medical treatment, physical exercises and medicine. Furthermore, several of the interviewed parents regularly had to get up at night, for example, to turn the child in bed, check the child's breathing and give water and medicine ("For 23 years I've been up several times every night").

It is necessary to summarise these stories by noting that the ideological turn in disability policy towards normalisation and integration – although within the realm of a strong, lingering medical view – was welcomed and embraced by these parents, and many of them had chosen to take on the care responsibility it entailed. However, this must be related to the fact that the scope of the reforms was perceived as rather limited, and services from the health and social care sector were also considered insufficient, failing to give the families adequate support adjusted to their specific care needs and life situation. Instead, all the parents described having to rely completely on their own personal, financial, emotional and social resources.

Letting go

Another central event in the child's life, also of crucial significance to the parents, was the transition into adulthood, which involved liberation, leaving the parents' home, and becoming independent. To the parents, the goal had been for the child to find her or his own home, a job or some other meaningful activity, and also opportunities to live an independent life, not least according to the disability discourse on independence, citizenship and participation (see Bjarnason, 2002). From having had complete responsibility for the child, including in terms of care, for many years, the time had come for them to 'let go' and leave the (care) responsibility to others, to the adult child, the social services, health insurance, doctors, assistants and so on.

To the parents, however, this transition highlighted a number of obstacles and dilemmas. An insight encountered was that their *role as parents* was given new meaning in relation to the adult child when their responsibility as *caregiver* did not end as expected. Difficulties in finding a good, properly adapted home, and in finding and coordinating assistance, made the parents realise that they would continue to play a central role as caregivers in the life of the adult child. Several of the interviewees tried to describe the way their parenthood differed from other parents (with non-disabled adult children), and they used the word 'adult parenthood' to emphasise this fact, as exemplified in the following quotation:

> 'I usually talk about the parenthood that never ends, it's always there, an adult parenthood. There is always a worry about it, and I want to get rid of it, but there is no one to pass it on to, no one who wants to take over the baton. That's how I feel about it.'

Some parents claimed that due to this transition – and despite rigorous preparations – a number of difficulties had become apparent. These difficulties can be partly explained by the fact that the transition into adulthood also implies a transition from a more well-organised 'children's' medicine – the social care and rehabilitation system – into the ordinary 'adult' health and social care systems. These were perceived as lacking coordination, continuity and stability, often with a worse situation socially and health-wise, which had devastating consequences for the adult child's everyday life. Additionally, the difficulties sometimes arose because several of the children had severe impairments, sometimes implying communicative but also certain cognitive difficulties which meant that they needed help with their finances, and with dealing with authorities, health and social care administrators, and so on.

Their extensive disabilities, together with difficulties speaking for themselves and claiming their rights in certain situations, had limited their possibilities of reaching full independence, according to the parents. These limitations often clashed with the high expectations and the rhetoric within the 'disability field' (policy, research, practice, disability movement), which emphasises independence, influence and power of action. The next excerpt gives a good illustration of this:

> 'Now they say, [at social services] "He's a grown-up man now, he can speak for himself." Yes, that's true but still he's got his communicative problems and he *can't* speak for himself. /.../ "But he has to take care of his finances," they say. He's got a few thousand every month which he handles fine, but if I said to him that he has to take care of this and this and this as well, it would turn into chaos. He can't manage that.'

A common experience among the parents was that they were criticised for being over-protective, unable to let go and hindering their children from becoming free and independent (see also Brett, 2002; Goodley, 2003; Shakespeare, 2006). But this is partly a simplistic picture and partly a picture in which the parents do not recognise themselves. As one of the parents explained:

> 'When I accompany my other children to something, and support them I'm looked at as a great mum, a resource. But when I go with my [disabled] son I'm regarded as a burden, over-protective, someone who doesn't let go of him /.../ I'm never allowed to feel that I am a good mum ... when I meet administrators, assistants, no never. I'm just a demanding machine ... and from their perspective it's not even certain I want the best for him.'

The parents claimed they were faced by a similar mistrust from some of the activists and representatives in the disability movement and organisations. The following quote illustrates some of these perceived problems:

> 'Many of the activists within the disability movement say that we as parents don't have any right to speak for our [adult] children. We are only supposed to bring them up. Some say that we do more harm to our children, that we make everything a misery and complain ... But our children often have complex disabilities, and we have taken care of them from the start and at the same time try to live ordinary lives, work and make a living – they have no understanding and insight into this – it is very painful.'

On the contrary, the parents saw themselves as providing indispensable support for the adult child. They advocated for their rights and had tried to enable them to make a successful transition to adulthood and to live as independent and normal a life as possible.

1993/94 and the assistance reform

Of all Swedish disability reforms during the last decades none is ascribed such significance to the parents and their children as the 1993 Act concerning Support and Service for Persons with Certain Functional Impairments, implemented in 1994. The parents described this reform as a major turning point in their and their children's' lives. To some the law was implemented long after the child had grown into an adult and left home; To others the right to assistance became a reality while the child still lived at home, which meant they could have a new kind of family life that would have been impossible to achieve before. All parents agreed that this Act had led to an immense increase in quality of life, not least for the child ("He wouldn't be able to live the life he has now without his assistants"), but it had also increased the quality of social relationships inside and outside the family. The reform had without doubt led to increased freedom, safety and influence and power over the care and services. To some of the parents the reform had made it possible for them to work as assistants, or to coordinate the assistance for the adult child. This was a solution some found preferable, not least in the child's transitional phase to adulthood.

However, over the years, the parents had encountered other dilemmas related to the assistance they received: the influence, freedom and power had a price, namely, the loss of personal integrity and privacy, not only of the child, but also of the family.

> 'The reform has meant everything, incredible /.../ but – [*whispering*] you hardly dare to say this – the difficulties of living with assistants all the time, in your own home, it's not easy, it's not fun at all. Strangers in your own home all the time.'

Many parents claimed that the intentions of the reform, which included greater power, influence and responsibility over the assistance, were coupled with a kind of naivety which meant that to some disabled individuals the responsibility became too great. Their stories reveal difficulties in employing the right assistants ("He hired people because he felt sorry for them"), being an employer without exceeding one's power ("One day she just fired them all"), or preventing the assistants from 'taking over' ("She can't say no, so they decide everything for her"). The parents emphasised the importance of seeing the disabled person as a unique individual, who sometimes did not have the capacity to administer, employ and lead personal assistants. Additionally, to find the right organisational arrangement for the assistance was a long process, and these challenges had led to a more active role for the parents than they had expected.

The care responsibility in later life

An unexpected finding was that the parents – some of whom had reached quite an old age (80+) – still had a huge care responsibility and gave help and support of considerable proportions to their adult disabled children, sometimes despite a full range of support from public services, for example, personal assistance 24 hours a day. The following section focuses on the parents' care responsibility *today*. This lasting responsibility must be seen in light of the extensive care work carried out by parents during the childhood and young years of the disabled child in an era of extensive disability reforms and social changes.

Different caring roles

Different caring roles played by parents emerged in the interviews; Some worked as personal assistants, others advocated for their children since they were too impaired to speak for themselves. All had the role of being on standby duty day and night. A quite typical care situation for the parents in the study is illustrated by this retired mother, aged 67, of a daughter in her thirties:

> 'I'm legal custodian to my daughter, but I also step in for a few hours as assistant now and then, but I try to avoid doing that, because I can't cope any longer and I don't think I should. She is 33 years old now, and I just want to be her mother.... I take care of her finances and I'm trying to find someone else to take over that but it's not easy.'

This quote illustrates the wide range of care responsibility that can exist. This mother emphasised that she wanted to have a normal relationship with her daughter, and to hand over the responsibility to others. To *release yourself from the care responsibility* was a recurrent theme in the interviews, in particular among the older parents. A 75-year-old and retired father chose to move to another town as a way to escape from the lifelong care:

> 'She wants to manage on her own, but she also realises that she can't. And that's why she has turned to me. And she still does, but to a lesser extent. And I said "I won't leave you because I move. If you need help I'll be there for you." [*But the move was still important to you?*] 'Yes, that's right, as I said, I have been on duty 24/7 for 37 years.'

Others had chosen to keep a more active care role: a full-time working mother of a 35 year-old daughter stayed three nights a week (as a personal assistant) at her daughter's house, and took care of everything concerned with her finances, clothes, most of her technical advice, and she also helped her daughter at nights. All of the parents had what they described as a 'day and night duty'. They were (and had always been) constantly prepared to step in when needed: when assistants did not show up or got sick. With this day and night duty followed a state of being constrained, which had an impact on the parents' own life and acting space. Beside the practical care, parents described having a *total emotional responsibility* despite the fact that the adult child had personal assistants and services day and night:

> 'My son is a grown-up now, but I think about him every day. Whatever I do I think: "How is he? Who's working?" Now when the weather is warm "do they [the assistants] give him enough water?", and so on. So I care about him all the time.'

A further common role described by the parents was the caring role as 'mediator'. This role entailed demanding contacts with various authorities, writing letters of applications, appeal decisions, making reservations with doctors, occupational therapists and administrators, to mention just some examples. Again, this role was also associated with strong ambivalence. On the one hand the parents' ambition was to prepare the child to manage this on her or his own. On the other hand they constantly experienced how the child was treated worse, had to wait longer and had more difficulty claiming her or his rights when doing it her/himself. The involvement of the parents often seemed to facilitate and hasten different processes. The parents also wanted to protect their children – although adult today – from bad treatment, discriminating behaviour, time-consuming and sometimes humiliating situations and processes involving the authorities ("His time is too valuable to be spent on these exhausting contacts").

This caring responsibility – and the various caring roles – was also an unavoidable part of the 'adult parenthood' in later life, according to some of the parents. Others described this caring situation as unacceptable and increasingly as getting worse, but they said that no alternatives were available at present (Hallum and Krumbolz, 1993). The parents' descriptions of lifelong care responsibility illuminate the paradoxical expectations they meet as parents, including in later life. They are expected to be there, to step in and take over when the public help and support fail, while at the same time they experience being mistrusted, ignored and excluded:

> 'I don't have any disabilities, I don't have anything, sort of, I only have ... my parental competence, and that doesn't count. But I think I have as much competence and even more in different ways as they [the activists and representatives of disability organisations] have. I can move, I can walk and all that, sure, but my son's disability is under my skin.'

Impact on parents' life and later life

What kind of impact does this experience have on the parents' *own* lives? And how do parents view their own lifecourse in relation to this experience? Above all and in a general sense this experience has an impact on the total existence of the parents that is almost impossible for them to put into words:

> 'It has shaped me completely, in everything /.../ no, I can't explain,
> it is so throughout, it's life, what's important in life.'

When trying to be more specific the parents often described their lives as quite *atypical* in comparison to other parents in the same age or in the same life phase. Correspondingly, they found their parenthood to be quite different from the 'normal' parenthood. The *atypical* is partly represented by the care responsibility that extends above perceived normal parenthood; And it is partly represented by the shared experience of social barriers, discrimination, prejudices and poor service provision. Interestingly the parents thought that their atypical lifecourse had become more salient with ageing, and with becoming older. With declining health, when close friends and relatives had grandchildren, when it became clear that they could not expect any practical support and care from the child when needed in later life, it became obvious that their lifecourse had not followed the normative timetable or social roles associated with notions about the 'normal' lifecourse.

Seen from a lifecourse perspective, this experience of care responsibility for a disabled child has had other tangible effects on the life of the parent. The unstable and unreliable character of the disability/impairment over time – illness complications set in and the health condition might worsen with increased age (see also Chapter Two) – was a factor strongly influencing the parents' lives, and their care responsibilities. The parents described, for example, the impact this experience had had on their working life. Working part time was quite common among the parents when their children were small, but several stated that they had never been able to work full time, since they had sometimes chosen and sometimes had felt obliged to continue their caring responsibility. Linking these experiences with ageing and later life, it became clear from the interviews that part-time jobs and low income throughout the years had led to low pensionable income. Others, on the contrary, had chosen to work full time as a conscious strategy to retain a 'normal' life, to maintain relations ("I think that's why we are still married, both of us continued working full time"), and not least in order to free the child from guilt:

> 'I understood somehow that if I was to cope with all this I must have
> another life as well /.../ That has also meant that I have freed my son
> from the feeling that I have sacrificed myself for him.'

Working full time did not mean that the parents were released from care responsibility for the rest of the day or night. The experience of disability sometimes also led the parents into various professions/occupations within the disability field. Not surprisingly, several of the parents had been and still are involved with different parents' associations and disability organisations or are politically committed within the disability field. An important motive was to gain influence and contribute to a change in the life conditions for people with disabilities and their families.

> 'To me this engagement, or commitment, that's what matters, to me, to my son, to our family. For all the families to come, I have to work for changed attitudes and for better support for families with children with disabilities. Then I can think that my life or my son's life, are not in vain, in some way. That we have made a difference....'

Being engaged in these organisations could also provide opportunities for giving and receiving support. All parents emphasised the significance of having received support through these organisations while the children were small. To meet other families in the same situation was described as being valuable at that time. This kind of support was also needed and highly appreciated today, when the children had turned adult and left the parents' home. To meet other parents and to share experiences associated with the 'adult parenthood' was described as very important, and several emphasised the significance of receiving this kind of peer support in different life phases, including in later life (also see Chapter Two).

Together with other strains and trials in life, this lifelong care responsibility had in some cases contributed to poor health, and some parents described how these conditions had put a great strain on family relations, a result also found in earlier studies (Seltzer and Greenberg, 2001). Being a salient theme in their stories, it must be understood that it was not the child's impairments or the care responsibility *per se* that were perceived to be a burden or as causing distress and hardship in the parents' lives. Rather it was a result of perceived and shared experience of social barriers, and discrimination, together with poor support provision (see Dowling and Dolan, 2001). The interviewed parents also put strong emphasis on the fact that their untypical and partly different lives had not become 'bad lives' in any sense. On the contrary, their somewhat altered lifecourses also implied a rich life:

> 'Of course, if we compare ourselves with ... well, friends and others, we've got a completely different life /.../, we realise now. But we are not bitter, thinking our life is worse. No, we've got an incredible life, a very rich life because we've been so engaged and active.'

Ageing and death – worries about future care

Thoughts about the future – including issues of ageing and death – appeared to be fearful themes among the parents (Hallum and Krumboltz, 1993). Ageing inevitably entails certain limitations and changes in various ways. In the case of providing care for their disabled adult children, the parents' ageing itself imposed limitations on caring abilities (see also Jennings, 1987; Pillemer and Suitor, 1991). For several of them, their ageing process had become obvious and manifested itself in poorer physical health condition, for example, they suffered fatigue and lack of strength. Some expressed grief that they could no longer help the child with certain things. Additionally, the fear regarding these issues may be an acknowledgement from the parents' side that not only were they ageing, but *their children were ageing too*. They were possibly even more concerned about the ageing of the disabled child, describing an accelerating ageing progress with rapidly decreasing physical health, as this mother of a 40-year-old daughter said:

> 'Her legs have become worse, yes that has changed. And my partner, we've been together for five years now, he says "It's a bit sad in these five years to see the rapid decline." She was much more mobile at the beginning.'

Indeed, this fact brings up new ambiguities about how the children's continued life, disability with ageing and social needs should be managed by increasingly ageing parents who fear leaving these new and challenging responsibilities behind (Mengel et al, 1996). With this grows the emergence of worries about *future care*. Some of the parents, in particular those in their seventies and eighties, tried to plan for the future. The disabilities, the impairments and prognosis, together with the ageing process, made the future uncertain and frightening. This worry was compounded by the fact that some of the parents were well aware that their children – due to their complex impairments and disabilities – would never reach full independence. What would happen to their child's care after death was thus an issue that worried ageing caregiving parents. This was a pertinent concern; however, some satisfaction and peace of mind could be gained if non-disabled siblings or other close relatives could be expected to be the future caregivers (Pruchno et al, 1996). Among the parents, more or less explicit hopes and expectations were found that siblings or other family members would "take over":

> [*What will happen when you're no longer around? Do you think of that sometimes?*] 'Yes, absolutely /.../ I do feel a great comfort that he's got his sister. She's just incredible. She's a solid rock in life, and she will always stand up for her little brother and never give up.'

However, this might not be always the case, and the ageing and death of the parents might also be a cause of worry for those next in line: who to entrust with the care responsibility? All of the parents stated in the interviews that they could not die – who would then take over the care responsibility? This thought was closely linked with the uncertainty and concern about the life and care situation of the adult child in the future. Despite the efforts and planning for a safer and secure future for the adult child, there was much that the parents could not change or influence. In those cases, powerlessness and resignation could be discerned:

> [*What do you feel about the future?*] 'The future, what is that?' [*Is it hard to think about?*] 'Yes it is, because I consider it a dead end, actually.

> There are a lot of things I can't find any solution for; I can only rely
> on the hope that my daughter will have a good life; That there will be
> good people around her. That's all that matters, but I have no power
> or influence over that. I can only do my best.'

Thus, in some of the interviews there emerged a morbid desire of the parents for
their child to die before they did). These wishes – also found in earlier studies
(Grant, 1990; Hallum and Krumbolz, 1993) – reflect in the deepest way parents'
fears about their own death and its consequences for the adult child's continued
life and care.

Conclusion

In this chapter, ageing parents' experiences of having closely followed a disabled
child through the lifecourse were described. Their retrospectives reveal a lifelong
care responsibility that continues after the child has become adult and left the
parents' home. 'Adult parenthood' was a concept used by some of the interviewees
to emphasise the special experiences associated with having a disabled (adult) child.
This was an experience that had come to shape the parents' lifecourses. It also
had a huge impact on these parents' lives, privately, and sometimes professionally.
The choice of profession, working life and sometimes lifelong involvement in
various disability organisations are examples.

A conclusion that can be drawn from the interviews is that various disability
reforms and other social changes over the decades have had quite small effects
on the parents' life stories. The range of the reforms and support systems were
perceived as being limited, which frequently led to the parents having an extensive
and lasting care responsibility over the years. The only two reforms that seem to
have had a true (and long-term) impact on the parents' lives and their disabled
children's lives were the de-institutionalisation process during the 1960s and 1970s,
and later, the assistance reform of 1993. These reforms were described as having
made it possible for disabled people (and their families) to live a life like others,
maybe for the first time in history. At the same time, the parents highlighted
the challenges associated with living with and taking care of a disabled child, as
well as living with personal assistants. In the light of this, the parents' care role
and responsibility continued to be far more significant than they would wish
and expect.

Another conclusion is that the parents' lives were marked by the comprehensive
caregiving and care responsibility throughout the years, and also during the adult
years of the child. Therefore, the parents' accounts could be characterised as *care
biographies*. In spite of welfare state arrangements and reforms aimed at enhancing
the autonomy of disabled people, it seems clear that informal helpgivers, usually
family members, still played a key role in the everyday lives of these groups – as
for these parents. This caring responsibility and the various caring roles together
formed an unavoidable part of the 'adult parenthood' in later life, according to

some of the parents. The awareness of an uncertain future, together with fear about issues related to ageing and death, meant that these parents' care responsibilities also extended into the future.

A common experience among parents was that of being blamed for being overprotective of their children. Their experience of the welfare society and the public care sector often failing to take care of (young) adult people with disabilities led to doubts among the parents about the formal care system. At the same time, experiencing mistrust from parts of the disability movement and being disempowered by professionals was perceived by the parents as almost unbearable. The fact that parents could actually be a resource, and *act in alliance* with the disabled adult child, seemed impossible to combine with the discursive image of the disabled individual as independent – and this includes being independent from its family. Paradoxically, at the same time, the parents had a huge and implicitly expected – and not always self-assumed – care responsibility for the child as an adult. This seemed to be quite all right as long as we did not talk about it. This in turn contributed to a masking of the living conditions of not only the ageing family carers but possibly more importantly, of the lives of disabled people. This ambiguous position was also associated with dilemmas for the parents: how did family members relate to the quest for independence of the disabled person while he/she at the same time needed additional care and support? How could they combine supporting autonomy/independence with having care responsibility?

Their stories further revealed a (lifelong) lack of support for parents in their caring role. Within the realm of de-institutionalisation, 'normalisation' and 'integration', these families seem to have been very much left alone with a profound care responsibility, and had had to rely on their own personal resources. Although there has been rapid development in support for carers in recent years, it seems to have bypassed this group of carers. The lack of support was a recurrent theme in their lives, but it is possible that belonging to a group of carers not fitting the pre-assumed care profile (being a caring partner or a child to an old person with dementia), which is a narrow carer profile, might have reinforced the feelings of being ignored and made invisible as a family carer.

During the course of a long life with a child with severe disabilities and an unstable body, a complex parenthood emerges, shaped by experiences and circumstances that are often *shared* with the child. The quotation at the beginning of this chapter is an illustration of the experience that non-disabled family members, through their shared experience with the disabled child, can actually perceive themselves and the whole family as disabled. Yet the significance of close relationships and of families' and parents' roles as carers for people with disabilities seems difficult to reconcile with the disability discourse on autonomy and independence. The right to be independent, including independence from your family, easily becomes a worn-out catchphrase in the light of the filial/moral obligations and the interdependency expressed by the interviewees as part of reciprocal relationships. In the eagerness of disability policy to achieve autonomy, influence, participation, citizenship and so on, the significance of the family has come not only to be ignored but above all to be associated with something negative. The issues described in this chapter highlight the role of the family as far more important than has been acknowledged, and illustrate the relational ground and the interdependence on which family relations are based. Furthermore, the lifecourse perspective illuminates how issues such as parenthood, family and care are closely linked with disability, and become increasingly important *over time*.

References

Alwin, D.E. (1995) 'Taking time seriously: studying social change, social structure, and human lives', in P. Moen, G.H. Elder Jr and K. Lüscher (eds) *Examining lives in context: Perspectives on the ecology of human development*, Washington, DC: American Psychological Association, pp 211-62.

Avery, D.M. (1999) 'Talking "tragedy": identity issues in the parental story of disability', in M. Corker and S. French (eds) *Disability discourse*, Buckingham: Open University Press, pp 116-26.

Bjarnason, D.S. (2002) 'New voices in Iceland. Parents and adult children: juggling supports and choices in time and space', *Disability & Society*, vol 17, no 3, pp 307-26.

Borsay, A. (1990) 'Disability and attitudes to family care in Britain: towards a sociological perspective', *Disability, Handicap & Society*, vol 5, no 2, pp 107-22.

Brett, J. (2002) 'The experience of disability from the perspective of parents of children with profound impairment: is it time for an alternative model of disability?', *Disability & Society*, vol 17, no 7, pp 825-43.

Bury, M. (1982) 'Chronic illness as biographical disruption', *Sociology of Health and Illness*, vol 4, no 2, pp 167-82.

DeMarle, D. and le Roux, P. (2001) 'The life cycle and disability: Experiences of discontinuity in child and family development', *Journal of Loss & Trauma*, vol 6, no 1, pp 29-43.

Dew, A., Llewellyn, G. and Balandin S. (2004) 'Post-parental care: a new generation of sibling-carers', *Journal of Intellectual & Developmental Disability*, vol 29, no 2, pp 176-9.

Dowling, M. and Dolan, L. (2001) 'Families with children with disabilities – inequalities and the social model', *Disability & Society*, vol 16, no 1, pp 21-35.

Eurofamcare (2009) *Services for supporting family carers of older dependents in Europe: Characteristics, coverage and use*, The Trans-European Survey Report. Deliverable No 19, Hamburg: Eurofamcare, LIT.

Fyhr, G. (2002) *Den 'förbjudna' sorgen: Om förväntningar och sorg kring det funktionshindrade barnet* [*The 'forbidden' grief: On expectations and grief for the disabled child*], Stockholm: Svenska föreningen för psykisk hälsa (Sfph).

Giele, J.Z. and Elder, G.H. Jr (1998) 'Life course research: development of a field', in J.Z. Giele and G.H. Elder Jr (eds) *Methods of life course research: Qualitative and quantitative approaches*, Thousand Oaks, CA: Sage Publications, pp 5-27.

Glucksmann, M. (2006) 'Developing an economic sociology of care and rights', in L. Morris (ed) *Rights: Sociological perspectives*, London: Routledge, pp 55-72.

Goodley, D. (2003) 'Against a politics of victimisation: disability culture and self-advocates with learning difficulties', in S. Riddell and N. Watson (eds) *Disability, culture and identity*, Harlow: Pearson, pp 105-30.

Government Bill (1999/2000:79) *Action plan for disability policies*, Stockholm: Ministry of Health and Social Affairs.

Grant, G. (1990) 'Elderly parents with handicapped children: Anticipating the future', *Journal of Aging Studies*, vol 4, no 4, pp 359-75.

Greenberg, J., Seltzer, M. and Greenly, J. (1993) 'Aging parents of adults with disabilities: Their gratifications and frustrations of later-life caregiving', *Gerontologist*, vol 33, no 4, pp 542-50.

Gubrium, J. (1995) 'Taking stock', *Qualitative Health Research*, vol 5, no 3, pp 267-9.

Gustavsson, A. (1998) *Inifrån utanförskapet. Om att var annorlunda och delaktig* [*Exclusion from within*], Stockholm: Johansson & Skyttmo förlag.

Hallum, A. and Krumbolz, J. (1993) 'Parents caring for young adults with severe physical disabilities: psychological issues', *Developmental Medicine & Child Neurology*, vol 35, no 1, pp 24-32.

Hansson, J.-H., Jegermalm, M. and Whitaker, A. (2000) *Att ge och ta emot hjälp. Anhöriginsatser för äldre och anhörigstöd – En kunskapsöversikt* [*To give and to receive help. Family caregiving to older people and support for caregivers – A review of literature*], Stockholm: Ersta Sköndal University College.

Jarkman, K. (1996) *Ett liv att leva. Om familjer, funktionshinder och vardagens villkor* [*A life to live. Families, disability and everyday life*], Stockholm: Carlssons.

Jennings, J. (1987) 'Elderly parents as caregivers for their adult dependent children', *Social Work*, vol 32, no 5, pp 430-3.

Jeppsson Grassman, E., Whitaker, A. and Taghizadeh Larsson, A. (2009) 'Family as failure. The role of informal help and caregivers', *Scandinavian Journal of Disability Research*, vol 11, no 1, pp 35-49.

Jokinen, N.S. and Brown, R.I. (2005) 'Family quality of life from the perspective of older parents', *Journal of Intellectual Disability Research*, vol 49, no 10, pp 789-93.

Keith, L. (1992) 'Who cares wins? Women, caring and disability', *Disability, Handicap & Society*, vol 7, no 2, pp 167-75.

Lamura, G., Döhner, H. and Kofahl, C. (eds) (2008) *Family carers of older people in Europe. A six-country comparative study*, Hamburg: Eurofamcare, LIT.

McConkey, R. (2005) 'Fair shares? Supporting families caring for adult persons with intellectual disabilities', *Journal of Intellectual Disability Research*, vol 49, no 8, pp 600-12.

McElwee, L. (2000) 'Barn med funktionshinder och deras familjer' ['Disabled children and their families'], in P. Brusén and L.-Ch. Hydén (eds) *Ett liv som andra. Livsvillkor för personer med funktionshinder* [*A life like others. Living conditions among disabled people*], Lund: Studentlitteratur, pp 116-31.

Mengel, M., Marcus, D. and Dunkle, R. (1996) '"What will happen to my child when I'm gone?" Support and education group for aging parents as caregivers', *Gerontologist*, vol 36, no 6, pp 816-20.

Morris, J. (1993) *Independent lives: Community care and disabled people*, Basingstoke and London: Macmillan.

Morris, J. (1997) 'Care or empowerment? A disability rights perspective', *Social Policy & Administration*, vol 31, no 1, pp 54-60.

Nirje, B. (1980) 'The normalization principle', in R. Flynn and K.E. Nitsch (eds) *Normalization, social integration and community services*, Baltimore, MD: University Park Press, pp 31-49.

Olsson, L.-E., Svedberg, L. and Jeppsson Grassman, E. (2005) *Medborgarnas insatser och engagemang i civilsamhället – Några grundläggande uppgifter från en ny befolkningsstudie. [A Swedish national survey of volunteering and informal help – And care giving 2005]*, Stockholm: Ministry of Justice.

Pillemer, K. and Suitor, J. (1991) '"Will I ever escape my child's problems?" Effects of adult children's problems on elderly parents', *Journal of Marriage and the Family*, vol 53, no 3, pp 585-94.

Pruchno, R., Patrick, J. and Burant, C. (1996) 'Aging woman and their children with chronic disabilities: Perceptions of sibling involvement and effects on well-being', *Family Relations*, vol 45, no 3, pp 318-26.

Ray, L. (2002) 'Parenting and childhood chronicity: Making visible the invisible work', *Journal of Pediatric Nursing*, vol 17, no 6, pp 424-38.

Read, J. (2000) *Disability, the family and society: Listening to mothers*, Buckingham: Open University Press.

Sand, A.-B. (2005) 'Informell äldreomsorg samt stöd till informella vårdare – en nordisk forskningsöversikt' ['Informal elder care and support for informal caregivers – a Nordic review of literature'], in M. Szebehely (ed) Äldreomsorgsforskning i Norden. *En kunskapsöversikt [Research on elder care in the Nordic countries. A review of literature]*, Tema Nord 2005:508, Copenhagen: Nordic Council of Ministers.

Seltzer, M. and Greenberg, J. (2001) 'Life course impacts of parenting a child with a disability', *American Journal of Mental Retardation*, vol 106, no 3, pp 265-86.

Shakespeare, T. (2006) *Disability rights and wrongs*, London: Routledge.

Statistics Sweden (1992) *Handikappade 1975-1989. Levnadsförhållanden [Disabled people 1975-1989. Living conditions]*, Report 74, Stockholm: Statistics Sweden.

Swedish Government Official Report (2001:56) *Funktionshinder och välfärd [Disability and welfare. A research anthology from the welfare commission]*, Stockholm: Fritzes.

Swedish Research Institute for Disability Policy (2005) *Levnadsnivåundersökning 2005. En rapport om levnadsnivån för rörelsehindrade, hörselskadade, döva och synskadade personer [Living conditions 2005. A report on living conditions for people with impaired mobility, deaf and visually impaired]*, Stockholm: Swedish Research Institute for Disability Policy (HANDU AB).

Todd, S. and Jones, S. (2005) 'Looking at the future and seeing the past: the challenge of the middle years of parenting a child with intellectual disabilities', *Journal of Intellectual Disability Research*, vol 49, no 6, pp 389-404.

SEVEN

Ageing and care among disabled couples

Cristina Joy Torgé

Introduction

Mr and Mrs Eriksson (born 1946 and 1940), married for 36 years, both have multiple diagnoses. Mr Eriksson has had a developmental disorder from a young age and also has chronic pain. His wife has lived with illness since 1974 and was diagnosed with Parkinson's disease 12 years ago. Before her Parkinson's diagnosis, she took more responsibility for managing her husband's illnesses. However, having become gradually worse, she became eligible for personal assistance. As we talked about how two people with disabilities can complement each other, we also ended up talking about future concerns. According to Swedish assistance legislation, Mrs Eriksson is not entitled to more assistance hours because she is over 65.[1] This causes her husband to reflect about future care when age and disability take their toll on them both:

Mrs Eriksson: 'And, yes. Oh, I thought that I wanted to help him. So I try, but it's hard.'

Mr Eriksson: 'I've been through so many trials and ordeals.'

Mrs Eriksson: 'It's so hard to help you now that I've got this disease.'

Mr Eriksson: 'Yes, I know. But I can rise to the occasion instead. I've been thinking about that we ... I mean, I have an easy time seeing connections, like in charts. That's why I think about things in advance. And I have a lot of thoughts about how it's going to be when – as in a lot of people with Parkinson's when they become older, that it becomes worse – how I'd be able to handle that. Because she only has assistance from eight in the morning to four in the afternoon. And at nights, maybe she can't go to the toilet by herself. You have incontinence, you wet the bed and the bed gets soiled.... You've been really good lately, but of course, if I don't get my sleep – if I wake up at two or four in the morning because you need help – I wouldn't get a whole night's sleep. And I can get really crazy in my head. And I'd try to sleep during the day. I think about such things. I'm that kind, who takes things out too soon.'

Disability not only affects the disabled person but also the disabled person's family, in terms of the physical and psychological work involved in illness management and the shaping of everyday tasks (Corbin and Strauss, 1988). But, as illustrated in the interview above, this presents a special situation in families where more than 'one person has a disability, and even more so when members simultaneously face the accelerated effects of disability and ageing. The everyday lives of the Erikssons are characterised by many care tasks, which involve both practical and emotional work, such as helping with going to the toilet, giving moral support and managing assistants. The fact that age can, and often has, brought illness complications to both of them also adds to the worry of future needs and capacities for caring. It may mean, for example, that help needs increase at the same time as the ability to care for one's partner also becomes limited. The dialogue shows how care concerns permeate the Erikssons' past, present and future as a couple growing old together with disabilities. Yet, in much of the academic writing on spousal care, it is often taken for granted that there is one disabled spouse and one non–disabled partner.

What this chapter aims to explore is how spousal care can be understood when intimate partners choose to live and age together in spite of long-term disabilities. I discuss the questions: does it make sense to simultaneously be dependent on help and care in everyday life and to consider oneself a caregiver? How is help and care manifested in a relationship where both have disabilities? How does ageing and disability trajectory affect the preconditions for spousal caring? This chapter is based on a qualitative study using interviews with nine couples aged 60 and over, whose lives have been marked by disability. They may have had disabilities from birth, such as those who had cerebral palsy (CP) or genetic diseases. Others acquired disability at younger ages through juvenile diabetes, polio or accidents. They may also have had disabilities in middle age, such as those diagnosed with multiple sclerosis (MS), rheumatic diseases or those who live with the effects of other occurrences such as stroke.

Method and structure

In the conjoint interviews with the couples, I was able to get a picture of reciprocity in their common life that may not have been easy to see if they were interviewed separately in the normative roles of 'caregiver' or 'care receiver'. Their interaction constituted data not easily obtainable through other methods because the interviewees could communicate with each other about their shared situation (Allan, 1980). As Valentine notes about the joint interview (1999, p 68), 'a process of negotiation and mediation takes place between couples in the production of a single collaborative account for the interviewer'. In the interviews, themes such as interdependence and the dynamic between change and reciprocity came out as the partners constructed a common story of how it was to live, care *for* and care *about* each other as they were both growing older, oftentimes with worsening disabilities.

This chapter revolves around the themes of care, disability, couplehood and ageing. The starting point is that studying couples like Mr and Mrs Eriksson is not just to investigate an empirically interesting group; it also contributes to the literature on disabled family carers and problematises traditional ways of defining care. Arguments for this are discussed in the next section. Thereafter follow some empirical examples from the interviews, illustrating the questions raised. Finally, I explore how this knowledge relates to gerontology and disability studies.

Studying an invisible group

Why study couples ageing with disabilities? First, little is known about how these groups live, despite a population of disabled people living and ageing together. In Sweden, about a third of disabled people live with a partner who also has disabilities (Swedish Research Institute for Disability Policy, 2005), and this doesn't seem unique. In 1990, 6.1 per cent of partnered families in the US reported that both had a disability (LaPlante et al, 1996). A decade later, as much as 25 per cent of households with disability in the US had two disabled family members, and 5.7 per cent had three or more disabled family members, which might also include disabled couples (Wang, 2005). Disability in couplehood can be attributed not only to the fact that same-age couples are likely to acquire disabilities as they grow older, but also because disabled people are now also more likely to enter relationships with other disabled people like them (La Plante et al, 1996). Changes in public opinion and other social changes has made it more likely for people with diagnoses such as CP or Down syndrome to engage in partnerships and marry (Miller and Morgan, 1980; Brown, 1996). These changes can be attributed to the increased life expectancy of disabled people as well as to the development of social models of disability that would likely lead to partnerships (Brown, 1996; Also see Chapter One). This makes sense in the light of the historical exclusion of disabled people from rites of passage to adult status such as marriage and having children (Hunt, 1998, p 8). The positive self-image emerging from self-organised disability movements has likely affected how disabled people form relationships and experience emotional, sexual and romantic life (Shakespeare et al, 1996).

The fact that there are families with more than one person with disabilities means that family members are also very likely to find themselves in a position of giving and receiving informal care. Yet, disabled people's situation of informal care has barely been explored (Prilleltensky, 2004; Jeppsson Grassman et al, 2009; See also Chapter Six). There is no reason to believe that families with disabilities will decrease through a time when people with disabilities and chronic illnesses are reaching higher ages, and lifecourse milestones such as marriage and partnership become less problematic for disabled people. In light of these changes, disabled couples have become a relevant group to study in that there may be unique considerations about care and ageing compared to other older couples.

Care as age- and function-coded

A second reason to explore this field is to problematise the place of *care* in relation to disability. In feminist care studies, the concept of care was traditionally bound with the care receiver's functional status. To distinguish care from other forms of relationship or obligation-based reciprocity such as servicing, the receiver's inability to do a task him or herself – and thereby his or her relationship of dependence – was central (Waerness, 1996; Daly and Lewis, 1998). 'Analytically, the distinction between caring for dependent persons who are not able to take care of themselves and caring for those who can manage well on their own remain important', write Leira and Saracendo (2002, p 62). Thus, feeding or bathing a young child or an old person count as care, but not when done to capable adults, even when this is done out of the same reasons such as love. Consequently, while having brought care to the academic and policy agenda, care research was also founded on a relationship of asymmetry, either in terms or health status, age, or both. The fundamental asymmetry in care relationships is not what is problematic; it is hard to deny that care is based on an acknowledgement of need (see Tronto, 1993; Shakespeare, 2000). What is problematic is how *this asymmetrical exchange is often conflated with certain relations regarding age and functioning*, that is, how certain ages and functional states become considered the grounds for a carer or dependant status.

This is evident in how policy issues often build on age- and function-coded norms and expectations. Formal care literature focuses on middle-aged care workers' wage and pension penalties that put them in a position of possibly not being able to afford good care when they themselves grow old (Ungerson, 2000; Evandrou and Glaser, 2003; England, 2005). Informal care literature uses the same age codes, for example, by focusing on the working-age 'sandwich generation' who take care of both the young and the elderly during their supposedly most productive work years. To consider old people simply as a care burden undermines their contributions as carers (Arber and Ginn, 1990). Yet interestingly, even this has led to a problem of 'caring for the carers'. The problem focus has thus shifted from older people as actual givers of care to framing them, together with young carers, as 'vulnerable groups in their own right', who carry a heavy burden when they should instead be supported (Wenger, 1990; Doran et al, 2003). These discussions appear to limit appropriate carers to the productive-aged and non-disabled. Further, the assumption that the young and old – supposedly receivers of care – are burdened by care tasks also assumes that it is ill and disabled people, regardless of age, who constitute the real caring burden.

Disabled people as 'care invisible'

The place of disabled people in care discourse should be problematised since at the same time that disability seems to be a central criterion for defining care, disabled people, in particular disabled adults, can be *care invisible*. By this I mean not only that disabled people usually become pigeonholed as dependants and often disqualified from the label of 'carer' (Thomas, 1997; Prilleltensky, 2004). Disabled adults' situation of receiving informal care is often also hidden behind a rhetoric of self-sufficiency despite impairments (Jeppsson Grassman et al, 2009). In contrast to the helpless child or frail elderly person who seem to be dependant because of age and functioning, cared-for role poses a threat to autonomy to the self-realising disabled adult (see Shakespeare, 2000). At the same time, disabled people's right to care may also be taken away from them (Keith and Morris, 1995; Thomas, 1997).

Care's ambivalent position in relation to disability studies says nothing about the *actual* caregiving that occurs, however. The UK Life Opportunities Survey (ONS, 2009) reported that more adults with impairment provided informal help within and outside the household than adults without impairment. People with impairments also provided longer caring hours (50+ hours a week). Likewise, the Australian Survey of Disability, Ageing and Carers (ABS, 2009) showed that over a third of all family carers aged 15 and over had disabilities themselves, and that 35 per cent of this group considered themselves as primary carers. It seems surprising that disabled people provide a lot of care, and often for longer periods of time. Do the reports aim to highlight invisible caregiving, or to show how disabled people are disproportionately *burdened* and possibly excluded from social life *because of caring*? This aside, these statistics show that people with disabilities do in fact engage in activities that they define as caring, contrasting with the absence of disabled carers in academic discourse. Care discourse had not been able to account for all experiences of care, and care in disability contexts remains to be explored. The next sections aim to do this through showing some results from the empirical study.

The lifecourse and everyday life

The data just described raises the question, whether it makes sense to simultaneously be dependent on care and also be a caregiver. It seems so from, for instance, my interview with Mr and Mrs Blom:

> I am interviewing the Bloms in their living room – I in the sofa and they in their wheelchairs. In the kitchen, their assistants wash and dry the lunch dishes. I ask the couple about their 40–50 years of living with MS. We talked about how they met each other after their diagnoses and how they ended up living together, initially without any formal help: 'We wanted to manage by ourselves.' The complications of

their MS, especially when Mrs Blom lost the ability to eat by herself, resulted for the need for both of them to apply for assistance. Their assistants help them with their daily activities, but Mr Blom – 10 years his wife's senior but more mobile – still provides indispensable help every day, most notably for his wife's most intimate care needs when they are alone.

Interviewer: 'Before I go to the next questions, I want to hear how an ordinary day looks like.'''

Mr Blom: 'Sure thing.... About four, five, six, either [she] or I get up.'

Interviewer: 'So early?'

Mr Blom: 'Yes, yes, yes.'

Mrs Blom: 'Tell her!' [*giggles*]

Mr Blom: [*whispers*] 'She needs to pee! [*normal tone*] So I take away the warmer over your legs, and I help [her] out, back her out and into the toilet and.... Well, otherwise she's there by herself. And I wait a bit and look out the window until she's done. Then I help [her] into bed and go to the toilet myself. We go back and I turn on the lights if it's needed, and then we listen to the news.'

Mrs Blom: 'Then we sleep again.'

Mr Blom: 'When the international news comes on, we turn off the radio, we nap again, and the assistants come at eight or nine or at the arranged time. Mondays at 7.30.'

On first seeing the Bloms, assistance is their most obvious source of everyday help. As with many of the interviewed couples, living together despite severe disability and frequent hospital visits is sometimes not possible without this supporting environment. Couplehood in this case is not a closed dyad. On the contrary, it is made possible by different forms of formal help, including assistance for the blind, special transport services, assistive devices, home adaptations and home help. Some, like the Bloms, also qualified for personal assistance. Assistance in particular was an important condition for being able to live as a couple "like others", underlining how the social and historical interact with personal circumstances of disabled people. This contrasts, for example, with the US debate on 'marriage penalties' or losing disability benefits when partnered, which forces disabled people to hide or break off their relationships (Martin et al, 1995; Gill, 1996; Fiduccia, 2000).

On the one hand, assistance allows the couples independence from each other and frees them from heavy care responsibilities. But on the other hand, in a day already marked by the helping hands of assistants, instrumental caring can also become an important physical manifestation of *caring about* each other as intimate partners. The ability and *the choice* to be able to help each other seem important in maintaining the integrity of couplehood, especially when the rest of the day is characterised by formal help. Notably, Mrs Blom was eligible to apply for increased assistance hours to relieve her husband of care tasks, but this was out of the question. The fact that Mr Blom helped her despite having assistants there was something that she repeatedly underlined in the interview.

> Mrs Blom: 'I'm at the activity centre then /.../ I also exercise sometimes.'

> Mr Blom: 'I run off and do other things.'

> Mrs Blom: 'So they fix things, and then the assistants – he has one too – prepare food. So we have help, but we help each other too. [He] has helped me a lot.'

> Interviewer: 'You don't go out without assistants, is that right?'

> Mr Blom: 'When we're out, then we always have an assistant with us, when we're out and about. It feels safer that way.'

> Mrs Blom: '[My husband] helps me out of the wheelchair and puts it in the car. /.../ That we have assistance, it's because I need a lot of help and [he] can't take on all of the help himself. So he's the "next help". But we do help each other a lot, we help each other.'

Caring for each other was often remarked as a cherished moment, which is something other couples also expressed. The Bloms talked about the nightly help routine very fondly. And at the end of the day, although their day had revolved around different kinds of help needs, they still maintained that they were "just like an ordinary couple". Again, assistance is relevant for making this possible, but it also denotes that emotional closeness – the *raison d'être* of the intimate partnership (see Parker, 1993) – could be the motivation for doing care tasks at all. Even when physical abilities to show sexual intimacy disappear with age and illness, the opportunities to give and receive care can consist of important aspects of togetherness.

> Interviewer: 'You've told me what the day looks like until the assistants go home. What happens next?'

Mrs Blom: 'You mean here?'

Interviewer: 'When you're by yourselves in the evenings.'

Mrs Blom: 'In the evenings, we watch TV.'

Mr Blom: 'We talk a little. Then, when we're tired, if there's not anything else to do, I put some toothpaste on for [her], and [she] brushes her teeth.'

Interviewer: [*to the wife*] 'So you can do that?'

Mrs Blom: 'Yes, but I can't lift my arm too much.'

Mr Blom: 'Yes, that's it.'

Mrs Blom: 'Then [he] helps me to bed. He helps me put on my slippers, my night slippers. I can't lie down by myself, but [he] has to help me.'

Mr Blom: 'To lift her feet.'

Mrs Blom: 'To lift my feet, yes, into the bed.'

Interviewer: [*to the husband*] 'You do this as you sit in your wheelchair?'

Mr Blom: 'Yes, it's not a problem. It's just a matter of....'

Mrs Blom: 'Yes, he helps me to bed. And then I listen to an audiobook /.../ So that's how our lives look like. Oftentimes we send the assistants home so we can get more time alone. A bit earlier. To be alone with each other in the evenings and have it cosy.'

Mr Blom: 'Yeah, like an ordinary couple. That's just how we have it.'

What the Bloms describe as their ordinary day is interesting from the perspective of a care discourse that is premised on dependence. They seem to be exercising something between servicing and care. Mr Eriksson (see earlier) gave expression for this too when he bantered that he "spoils [his wife] too much" by volunteering to do things she could do. Yet Mr Blom and Mr Eriksson are also carers in a traditional sense. Although not necessarily associating himself as his wife's carer, Mr Eriksson began to consider taking on care tasks more actively when his wife's Parkinson's disease "gets worse as [she] gets older". Mr Blom, although regarded by his wife as the "next help", was indispensable in making Mrs Blom's day work.

The reciprocity in the couples' everyday lives – "just making things work", as a number express – seems like a given feature of couplehood. Yet in practice this involves activities that we would otherwise think of as care tasks, such as helping in bathing, toileting, feeding, dressing or mobility, despite carers needing formal help themselves. If these couples are not exercising care, how are we to understand this unexplored activity?

Care work: everywhere but nowhere

It is interesting to note that the couples seemed to be ambivalent about whether 'care' applied to them in the relationship. Many of them related this concept to medicalised forms of caring, such as helping each other with remembering or administrating medicine, or alarming emergency response teams and family members in case of emergencies. This is perhaps since, as Keith and Morris (1995) describe, the concept of caring usually invokes a nuance of 'taking responsibility for' someone.

When confronted with the question of care for each other, care seemed invisible or at least less apparent in its everydayness. The question about care came unexpectedly, and a number of couples responded like the Westerberg couple, both 66 years old and wheelchair users. Mr Westerberg now feels the late effects of the polio he had had as a child. Mrs Westerberg has a rare genetic disease and has gradually lost the ability to walk. Their physical conditions have "steadily worsened" through the years and they have had to give up frequent travelling that they used to enjoy. Mr Westerberg, who recently needed a respirator at nights, also suspected that he would have to be connected to the machine for longer periods of the day as he got older. They lived without assistance and described managing this situation really well in contrast to older neighbours. In other parts of the interview, however, they said that they were "precisely at the edge of getting by". Helping each other, although part of their everyday life, was natural as it was necessary for everyday living. It was self-evident, and thus also went mostly unremarked:

> Interviewer: 'You seem to both be quite independent, although you also help each other in your relationship. [*The couple agree, they hum*]. How would you define caring in a relationship as a couple?'

> Mr Westerberg: 'Aah....'

> Mrs Westerberg: 'Do you mean care for each other?'

> Interviewer: 'Yes.'

> Mrs Westerberg: 'Aah [*long pause*]. I guess we *do* do that.'

Mr Westerberg: 'Yeees....'

Interviewer: 'How would you describe it in words?'

Mr Westerberg: 'It's the way you show that ... I mean.... We *do* help each other, quite much.'

Mrs Westerberg: 'And we're – how do you say it – united in spirit. We don't need to say something all the time. You kind of know what to do anyway. I mean, we've lived together for – how long? – We've known each other for 30 years.'

Mr Westerberg: 'Thirty years this year. That's right. Thirty years this year [*chuckles*], we've been together as a couple. And lived together for 22 years.'

Mrs Westerberg: 'Yes we have.'

Mr Westerberg: 'So of course you get to know each other well. She can tell what it is I need help with. She really does! And vice versa.'

This *everydayness* of care was also notable in the case of Mr and Mrs Dahl, 83 and 78 years respectively, who both had polio as children. The polio epidemic in 1940s Sweden had paralysed one of Mr Dahl's arms and Mrs Dahl's lower body. Aside from the initial disablement from polio, they had also acquired other health problems through the years. Both were hard of hearing (genetic in Mrs Dahl's case) and both also had had heart problems in the past year. Mrs Dahl suspected that "it must be all the negative stress" of living a long life with the effects of polio. When I asked them about what they needed help with, they were unable to think of anything but cleaning. Yet it soon appeared that Mr Dahl had in fact been helping his wife with showering. Lately, because of Mr Dahl's mild stroke, their daughter also had to help him with showering her: "With her and her Papa, it goes well."

At first, the couples did not think about regular provision of care for each other. The long life of disability, as well as a long time living together, appeared to obscure spousal care. First, the long life with disability meant that care and help were conditions for living, rather than momentary events. As one man said, "The times you pee are not something you think are extraordinary." Second, the long time living together also meant that reciprocity could grow to be part of the everyday routine. Involvement in care work was not necessarily something over and above the couples' regular division of tasks and their spousal interaction. The interviewed couples had been together for between four and 45 years. "In that way," remarked Mr Blom, "we've grown together and have learned how to combat our diagnoses." Perhaps this explains why spousal care, in the workaday world of these couples, had gone mostly unremarked. From their perspective, they were only interested in helping each other to "make things work".

The expression *making things work* recurred in a number of interviews when we talked about everyday life. This was especially true for couples before assistance, but also for couples who did not qualify for assistance today. Recalling the time without assistants, one said: "We helped each other with what we needed and didn't think much about it." Another expressed: "We help each other on all fronts so that it would work, but that doesn't have anything to do with our disabilities." The language of problem solving embedded in 'making things work' also implied, in their words, that the practical problems of living with disabilities "don't get solved by themselves" and "you don't get anything for free". Thus, there was a tangible *work* aspect in living together with disabilities and in keeping their lives as smooth-flowing as possible. Everyday life involved physical, emotional and communicative work. There were also many considerations such as where to get help when things *didn't* work, how to plan their chores around tiredness and increased fatigue, deciding which activities to sacrifice and which meaningful activities to sustain.

Visible and invisible care

Although the work aspect of care is hidden behind its everydayness, the actual care tasks are many. This indicates the many manifestations of care despite both partners living with disabilities. One couple using wheelchairs showered together in order to help each other with scrubbing. A man with an electric wheelchair "rolls away" to the grocery, so that his wife, also a wheelchair user, doesn't need to. A husband with one arm makes technical aids such as individually designed toothbrushes and peelers for his wife with a congenital disability. Another man, with 24-hour assistance and mobility and communication difficulties, escorts his partner who has difficulty walking to the bus stop. She, on the other hand, makes him food despite assistants there to help, so that "he would eat real food and not pre-fab junk."

Yet part of the work that also takes a lot of time and thought can be described as *invisible caring*, such as protecting the partner's interests or working as 'advocates' in meetings with health professionals and bureaucrats, for example, to get assistance hours, a quicker diagnosis, a second opinion or access to technical aids. Mrs Englund, who has had cerebral palsy from birth, describes how she tried to protect her partner's interests – and their privacy – from the assistants that came and went all hours of the day. Another form of invisible work includes 'looking out for' signs and symptoms of the other's health, as if in a state of readiness. This was especially true when couples had illnesses that could develop into emergencies, such as diabetes, where low blood sugar levels could lead to periods of coma during sleep. A woman with hearing impairments, before her cochlear implant, shared that it was worrying not being able to hear if her diabetic husband was having seizures at night. A blind diabetic couple also told me how smelling each other's breaths gave them clues to plummeting insulin levels. Even with couples with different disabilities, educating themselves about each other's symptoms was an important aspect of care work and readiness to respond. On the one hand, worrying for a partner's health seemed natural, but it was also important practically as partners were usually the first there to help.

It was not apparent in many cases where care work ended and couplehood began. Nevertheless, it is important not to romanticise these relationships. Despite its everydayness, care work need not be natural or easy. Just as other couple relationships, to be married to a disabled person like oneself does not only mean harmony (Gill, 1996), and it involves different practical demands. Gill (1996) related how disabled couples can sometimes be confronted with questions such as 'How will the two of your survive? How can you take care of each other?' Mr Eriksson, in describing his relationship with his wife, gave a hint to an answer, in a way that reveals everydayness of care and its nature as work: "It's the same with us as with many other couples. Just a tad more."

Time and embodiment

So far, I have discussed the themes of disability, couplehood and care from the interviews, but it is also relevant to explore implications over time, through increasing age. As Katz notes (2010, p 357), 'all research in gerontology begins with the body.' Likewise, to talk about ageing in these couples' contexts, it is inevitable to approach it through the lens of disabled ageing bodies. The ageing body/bodies means that the couples expect to deal – and sometimes already are dealing – with the undeniable concreteness of functional decline despite an independent life together. The projected misfortunes of older people were thought to soon be relevant for them (See Öberg and Tornstam, 2003) and they anticipated more practical difficulties due to their disabilities.

The fact that *making things work* is often dependent on physicality and timing discloses how the couples' care context was experienced as an *equilibrium*. Statements such as being "at the edge of getting by" or "taking things out too soon" express this sense of balance. The couples' care context works pretty well, but this balance is premised on bodies that work *for now*. The fact that physical changes in one or both of them could lead to dramatic consequences in their everyday life was something the couples bore witness to, and was especially salient in Mr Skogman's story about how the slow progression of disease, with unexpected outcomes, could lead to a change in living conditions. From being relatively independent despite disability, suddenly he and his wife both unable to do anything around the home for months:

> 'I got spinal stenosis some years back. / ... / You're in real pain. It had to be operated; it's the only way to make it go away. And you know how it is, out here in the countryside. It takes forever to get to a doctor / ... / Then it also takes forever to investigate the problem, and

it takes forever before the operation. It took about a year or so /.../
At the same time, I had a problem with my knee. It stopped working,
more or less. I had to have a prosthetic knee. Then, after a few years,
I slipped. I was kind of fumbling, since I can't really feel where my
feet are, so that added to it. It was winter, and slippery. So, I got a foot
fracture. And on that, I got a post-operative infection. /.../ So I was
at the hospital, and the bacteria turned out to be resistant to antibiotics.
So I had that infection for a half year. I got operated again and loads
of these sorts of things. Those things really take their toll. And then,
I was stuck in a chair. [My wife] had also just been operated then
on her foot. Three days after [her planned operation], that's when I
slipped and broke my foot. So we were just sitting, both of us in casts.'

The consequence of time and bodily change is that new problems eventually have
to be dealt with. As in the example above, this involves a long and constant process
of change. Changes involving disability trajectory, changed roles at retirement
or the ageing of the relatively more mobile spouse are anticipated. But there are
also changes that creep in, such as not knowing when tiredness kicks in, unseen
complications, difficulties due to the weather or unavailability of other helpers,
or concerns that formal care services might be taken away.

Because the care context is experienced as a balance, it is not surprising that
the couples had worries around future care. They worried for their own care
needs, but they also worried if they would have the future capacities to care for
their partners and to live as they did today. Mrs Englund, 64 at the time of the
interview, did not take her partner's 24-hour assistance for granted. She mistrusted
authorities and was wary of how budget cuts might affect the future conditions
of Mr Englund's assistance, since "I'm not that young either /.../ I'm afraid that
they might put demands on me that I won't be able to handle." Mrs Hammar,
who has 65 hours of assistance each week but receives help from her husband
for help when they are alone ("which is another thing"), also worried about
a time when circumstances might change. Thus, she was looking around for
other potential places to live: "I can't live in this house by myself. If my health
deteriorates, [Mr Hammar] can still manage things. My worsening disability has
nothing to do with this house. But it has something to do with [Mr Hammar's
health]. If something happens to him, it all gets affected."

These concerns tell of important dimensions in care that are usually neglected.
First, care concerns are not limited to present needs and what is obvious through
mere helping – of helping to feed, bathe, go to the toilet, shop – or even through
invisible work such as being an advocate or standing ready. Thinking about
care stretches both in the past and in the future. Consequently, when couples
assess their present care context as an equilibrium, they set this in contrast with
experiences, expectations – and sometimes even fears or hopefulness – of how it
is to live and age with disabilities together.

This relates to the second point of how these care concerns are *embodied* and strongly linked to the couples' awareness of temporality and disabled embodiment through the lifecourse. These are expressed by the Skogmans as they looked back on those few helpless months where care *didn't* work and by Mrs Englund and Hammar, as they regarded future possibilities and limitations where living and caring for each other *wouldn't* work. Disabled embodiment – and all the practical difficulties that this might mean for the couple – shape projections and actions of how to live, age and care for each other with increasing adaptations.

Third, in living everyday life together, these disabled couple's thoughts about care reveal in an exceptional way how changes that affect the individual body over time are not merely personal concerns, but are *shared concerns*. The most obvious of shared concerns are the practical issues of living, such as choice of housing, meeting needs, maintaining projects, mobilising informal help or saving for future care. But in a dyadic relationship, concerns about the individual body also become a shared concern. It existed in Mr Eriksson's worries about "getting crazy in his head" when having to help his wife to the toilet, or Mrs Englund's comment that "I'm not so young either," and fearing increased care responsibilities. Are these expressions of a burden perspective concerning a vulnerable group? Of disabled individuals fearing that they might be responsible for more care than they could provide? This view seems to be only half the story, for couples also expressed caring for each other as "another thing" and, despite formal help, *chose* to care and maintain a life together.

We-work

So how do we understand the caring relationship between these couples? One suggestion is a concept that I call *we-work*. This is proposed not as a synonym for care, because the care concept is not sufficient to understand these couples' situations. Rather, we-work is a concept to emphasise what these disabled couples do together to maintain living and ageing together, with all its practical considerations. To be disabled is "practically difficult", and living together with another person with disabilities also means that "you cannot take your partner's help for granted". Thus, we-work is an expression of what practical, emotional and care-related concerns it takes to maintain – not instrumental goals in the first hand, as it is with 'care', but a relationship between two people with disabilities. It includes everything that couples do and think to make things work and to maintain an equilibrium in their common life despite the knowledge of the unreliability of change. It has a normative dimension: the social and moral expectations of them as intimate partners, married or living together. This normative aspect can make we-work invisible. But although it has an affective dimension, it is not entirely something natural: we-work has a nature as work, wrapped around present and future care.

To merely consider care as a burden takes away aspects of caring that might be voluntary. These couples engage in we-work among other things because of a drive to make their common life work despite all its practical implications. This is why the burden perspective is not enough. The delineation between servicing and care is also an artificial distinction for these couples for whom both forms of reciprocity meld together.

Conclusion

This chapter set out to discuss how it is to age as a disabled couple and provide mutual care. First, does it make sense to simultaneously be dependent on help and care in everyday life and to consider oneself a caregiver? Despite a discourse that seems focused on healthy, middle-aged carers, the answer seems to be yes. It seems that a more nuanced view of care is needed in order to accommodate other meanings of 'care' than the mere instrumental helping of people who cannot help themselves. As these couples show, care also fulfils other purposes, such as maintaining closeness.

Second, how is help and care manifested in a relationship where both have disabilities? The interviews reveal that, like many other couples, caring activities are both practical and affective in nature. This reciprocity, however, is hidden both by norms of what couplehood entails and by the necessity of help in making everyday life work.

Third, how does ageing and the disability trajectory affect preconditions for caring? Caring is embodied as well as temporal and shared. In assessing their care today, the couples compared it with past experiences and future expectations that were also intimately linked with their disabled embodiment and preconditions for being able to age together with disabilities. As Becker writes,

> Embodiment encompasses individuals' historical, lived, experiences of their bodies, and this temporal dimension, especially between how the body has been experienced historically and expectations about the future of the body, affects responses to bodily changes. Past life experiences, including earlier illnesses, life transitions, and other major life events are central to current experiences of health and illness, as are expectations for the future. (Becker, 1994, p 62)

This takes on a special dimension when considering that everyday life and its concerns are shared between two people whose bodies are not seen to be stable or always predictable. Thus the care that they do in order to maintain everyday life and their relationship can perhaps best be understood as a kind of we–work that contains normative and work elements, but without which the relationship as a couple would not exist.

How can these insights on nine disabled couples be relevant for gerontology? There are, of course, parallels. Caring for a partner is an experience likely to be shared predominantly by older people who are themselves at an age where the risk of incurring disabilities is high (Corden and Hirst, 2011). In many cases, as in the younger couples interviewed by Parker (1993), it may be that both partners have a disability, but it is the chronology that decides which partner becomes labelled as 'carer' and which as 'disabled spouse'. Jegermalm (2006) also reported that those who provided personal care and other kinds of care like 'keeping company' and 'keeping an eye' were mostly older people, often wives.

Older spouse caregivers are said to engage in similar caring tasks, blurring traditional gender norms (Arber and Ginn, 1990). But because disability is never a fixed bodily state, patterns of caregiving between elderly husbands and wives can likewise vary over time as the spouses' disability improves or progresses (Noël-Miller, 2010). Older spouse carers can thus transition into more demanding caring roles, or return to a non-caregiving status (Burton et al, 2003). In the case of older spouses where the carer is also at a risk of having an impairment or already has a disability, transitions can mean that the very possibility of giving spousal help and care also changes over time. A sudden or expected change in any of the partners' health can in turn lead to considerable changes in the couples' care abilities and needs.

In spite of this, what effects care has on the life of the older couple *as a family unit* seems to be largely ignored. From the results of a systematic literature review conducted by Walker and Luszcz (2009), a majority of the spousal care literature still focuses on the individual impacts of caregiving, such as caregiver burden, while few studies investigate the impact of caregiving on the couple together. Borgermans and colleagues (2001, p 6) also remark on the growing care literature that this 'is dominated by a burden perspective, seldom including the positive aspects of caregiving. There is an apparent lack of practice literature, describing the dynamic nature and complexity of family caregiving.'

The insights from this study can also be relevant to disability studies, in that this study shows disabled people in caring and reciprocal roles. Many of the interviewed couples were members of disability organisations and talked about the right to be independent. Yet, caring, and even helping each other with necessary or intimate tasks, was not considered as oppositional to their struggle for self-determination. Rather, these were a natural part of their life as a "couple like others". This problematises different meanings of care, dependence and independence.

Through looking at care through a lifecourse perspective – for example, how assistance releases the care burden but also makes other expressions of care relevant – the study is also an example of how the personal and political intersect. This intersection also fits well with a person-in-environment perspective of growing old with disabilities: that ageing with a disability is influenced by the 'multi-layered social contexts in which people age, ranging from immediate micro worlds of family and friends, the meso-level of organisations and service systems to the macro social structure aspects of the society' (Hooyman and Kiyak, 1999, cited in Bigby, 2004, p 21). One observation has been that 'disability studies has downplayed the personal and focused on the structural. It seems almost as if disability studies have reproduced the wider split between public and private with which students of gender studies are familiar. Thus we learn much about the public lives of men and women but next to nothing about the private and personal lives of men or women' (Shakespeare et al, 1996, p 8). This study, by exploring the shared everyday lives of disabled couples and how they age together "just like others" shows, however, how care is not just a political question, but also a personal and interpersonal question.

Note

[1] Individuals with certain functional disabilities can be eligible for personal assistance after they turn 65 only if their application for assistance has been granted before their 65th birthday. The granted assistance hours may not be increased thereafter. They become, instead, eligible to home help service for help with emerging needs after the age of 65.

References

ABS (Australian Bureau of Statistics) (2009) *Disability, ageing and carers, Australia: Summary of findings*, Canberra: ABS.

Allan, G. (1980) 'A note on interviewing spouses together', *Journal of Marriage and the Family*, vol 42, pp 205-10.

Arber, S. and Ginn, J. (1990) 'The meaning of informal care: gender and the contribution of elderly people', *Ageing & Society*, vol 10, no 4, pp 429-54.

Becker, G. (1994) 'The oldest old: autonomy in the face of frailty', *Journal of Aging Studies*, vol 8, no 1, pp 59-76.

Bigby, C. (2004) *Ageing with a lifelong disability: A guide to practice, program and policy issues for human services professionals*, London: Jessica Kingsley Publishers.

Borgermans, L., Nolan, M. and Philip, I. (2001) 'Europe', in I. Philip (ed) *Family care of older people in Europe*, Amsterdam: IOS Press, pp 1-26.

Brown, R. (1996) 'Partnership and marriage in Down syndrome', *Down Syndrome Research and Practice*, vol 4, no 3, pp 96-9.

Burton, L., Zdaniuk, B., Schulz, R., Jackson, S. and Hirsch, C. (2003) 'Transitions in spousal caregiving', *The Gerontologist*, vol 43, no 2, pp 230-41.

Corbin, J. and Strauss, A. (1988) *Unending work and care*, San Francisco, CA: Jossey-Bass Publishers.

Corden, A. and Hirst, M. (2011) 'Partner care at the end-of-life: identity, language and characteristics', *Ageing & Society*, vol 31, no 2, pp 217-42.

Daly, M. and Lewis, J. (1998) 'Introduction: conceptualising social care in the contest of welfare state restructuring', in J. Lewis (ed) *Gender, social care and welfare state restructuring in Europe*, Aldershot: Ashgate, pp 1-24.

Doran, T., Drever, F. and Whitehead M (2003) 'Health of young and elderly informal carers: analysis of UK census data', *British Medical Journal*, vol 327, p 1388.

England, P. (2005) 'Emerging theories of care work', *Annual Review of Sociology*, vol 31, pp 381-99.

Evandrou, M. and Glaser, G. (2003) 'Combining work and family life: the pension penalty of caring', *Ageing & Society*, vol 23, no 5, pp 583-601.

Fiduccia, B.W. (2000) 'Current issues in sexuality and the disability movement', *Sexuality & Disability*, vol 18, no 3, pp 167-74.

Gill, C.J. (1996) 'Dating and relationship issues', *Sexuality & Disability*, vol 14, no 3, pp 183-90.

Hooyman, N. R. and Kiyak, H. A. (1999) *Social ggerontology: A multidisciplinary perspective,* Needham, MA: Allyn & Bacon.

Hunt, P. (1998) 'A critical condition', in T. Shakespeare (ed) *The disability reader: Social science perspectives*, London: Cassell, pp 7-19.

Jegermalm, M. (2006) 'Informal care in Sweden: a typology of care and caregivers', *International Journal of Social Welfare*, vol 15, no 4, pp 332-43.

Jeppsson Grassman, E., Whitaker, A. and Taghizadeh Larsson, A. (2009) 'Family as failure. The role of informal help-givers to disabled people in Sweden', *Scandinavian Journal of Disability*, vol 11, no 1, pp 35-49.

Katz, S. (2010) 'Sociocultural perspectives on ageing bodies', in D. Dannefer and C. Phillipson (eds) *The Sage handbook of social gerontology*, London: Sage Publications, pp 357-67.

Keith, L. and Morris, J. (1995) 'Easy targets: a disability rights perspective on the "children as carers" debate', *Critical Social Policy*, vol 15, no 44-45, pp 36-57.

LaPlante, M.P., Carlson, D., Kaye, H.S. and Bradsher, J.E. (1996) 'Families with disabilities in the United States', *Disability Statistics Report 8*, Washington, DC: US Department of Education, National Institute on Disability and Rehabilitation Research.

Leira, A. and Saracendo, C. (2002) 'Care: actors, relationships and contexts', in B. Hobson, J. Hobson, J. Lewis and B. Siim (eds) *Contested concepts in gender and social politics*, Cheltenham: Edward Elgar Publishing, pp 55-81.

Martin, D.A., Conely, R.W. and Noble, J.H. (1995) 'The ADA and disability benefits policy: some research topics and issues', *Journal of Disability Policy Studies*, vol 6, no 2 pp 1-15.

Miller, S. and Morgan, M. (1980) 'Marriage matters: for people with disabilities too', *Sexuality and Disability*, vol 3, no 3, pp 203-11.

Noël-Miller, C. (2010) 'Longitudinal changes in disabled husbands' and wives' receipt of care', *The Gerontologist*, vol 50, no 5, pp 681-93.

Öberg, P. and Tornstam, L. (2003) 'Attitudes toward embodied old age among Swedes', *International Journal of Aging and Human Development*, vol 56, no 2, pp 133-53.

ONS (Office for National Statistics) (2009) *UK Life Opportunities Survey*, Essex: UK Data Archive.

Parker, G. (1993) *With this body: Caring and disability in marriage*, Buckingham: Open University Press.

Prilleltensky, O. (2004) 'My child is not my carer: mothers with physical disabilities and the well being of children', *Disability & Society*, vol 19, no 3, pp 209-23.

Shakespeare, T. (2000) *Help*, Birmingham: Venture Press.

Shakespeare, T., Gillespie-Sells, K. and Davies, D. (1996) *The sexual politics of disability: Untold desires*, London: Cassell.

Swedish Research Institute for Disability Policy (2005) *Levnadsnivåundersökning 2005. En rapport om levnadsnivån för rörelsehindrade, hörselskadade, döva och synskadade personer* [*Living conditions 2005. A report on living conditions for people with impaired mobility, deaf and visually impaired*], Stockholm: Swedish Research Institute for Disability Policy (HANDU AB).

Thomas, C. (1997) 'The baby and the bath water: disabled women and motherhood in social context', *Sociology of Health and Illness*, vol 19, no 5, pp 622-43.

Tronto, J. (1993) *Moral boundaries: A political argument for an ethic of care*, New York: Routledge.

Ungerson, C. (2000) 'Thinking about the production and consumption of long-term care in Britain: does gender still matter?', *Journal of Social Policy*, vol 29, no 4, pp 623-43.

Valentine, G. (1999) 'Doing household research: interviewing couples together and apart', *Area*, vol 31, no 1, pp 67-74.

Waerness, K. (1996) 'The rationality of caring', in S. Gordon, P. Benner and N. Noddings (eds) *Caregiving: Readings in knowledge, practice, ethics, and politics*, Philadelphia, PA: University of Pennsylvania Press, pp 231-55.

Walker, R.B. and Luszcz, M.A. (2009) 'The health and relationship dynamics of late-life couples: a systematic review of the literature', *Ageing & Society*, vol 29, no 3, pp 455-80.

Wang, Q. (2005) 'Disability and American families: 2000', *Census 2000 Special Reports*, Washington, DC: US Census Bureau.

Wenger, G.C. (1990) 'Elderly carers: the need for appropriate intervention', *Ageing & Society*, vol 10, no 2, pp 197-219.

EIGHT

Living and ageing with disability: Summary and conclusion

Anna Whitaker and Eva Jeppsson Grassman

Introduction

This chapter gives a summary of the main results and perspectives presented in this volume, the aim of which was to discuss what it means to live a long life, to age and to become old for people who have disabilities acquired early in life. Key questions that have been discussed are: what does it mean to live a long life and age with a disability, either physical or mental? What are the implications of 'becoming old' for people who have had extensive disabilities for many years? What are the available formal and informal care resources? What does it mean to be an ageing parent and to continue to care for an adult disabled child? How are we to understand couplehood in the case when both parties are disabled? This book has adopted an overall lifecourse perspective when addressing these questions. Our intention in this final chapter is to point out the main contributions of the book, and to draw together some of the arguments presented to provide ideas for further development in the study of disability and ageing from a lifecourse perspective.

A long life with disability

How can we grasp what a long life with disability means? We have tried to explore this question from somewhat contrasting analytical perspectives and with different methodological approaches, and have found several answers rather than a single clear-cut one. An overall conclusion that can be drawn from the chapters in this book is that a long life with disability does not take one form but may have multiple shapes, depending on age at onset, time with disability, location in history, but also depending on the type and cause of the disability together with other factors such as socioeconomic position, whether the disability was visible or invisible, and societal attitudes surrounding it. We have underlined the relevance of the lifecourse approach since it can give insights into the illness and disability in its multiple shapes, and its impact *over time* on different phases of life. As we have seen in the various chapters, long lives with disability may also be permeated by particular types of involvement, such as political involvement, or by mutual caring roles, and, in the case of ageing parents, by caregiving over many years. Furthermore, the long lives with disability, described in the chapters, vary quite considerably in the extent to which they conform to modern ideals of well-compensated lives with disability. There is a great difference between the successful third-agers in Chapter Four, on the one hand, and the lives with illness described in Chapters Two, Five and Six, on the other – life with disability as it ought to be and life as it actually often seemed to be.

However, what people who live long lives and who age with disabilities *have in common* is that their lives differ in important ways from those of most other people – not least people of their own age and cohort. The disability has an impact on life phases and transitions and the fulfilment of life roles. The theme of work life and employment is one example. Some of the participants in the studies illustrate how the important transition into adulthood may be hampered by the impossibility of getting a job and fulfilling the work role. In other cases it was keeping the job and remaining in the work role that was the problem and which resulted in a premature transition into retirement. We have also seen (for instance, in Chapters Two and Five) how the illness or impairment and its disabling consequences may become so intrusive and exhausting that work is no longer experienced as meaningful, important or even possible, in spite of what is 'normal' for a given age. To be a spouse or a parent are other examples of adult roles that may be wished for but that sometimes seemed unattainable by the people with disabilities in our studies. Yet it is important to note that these roles, in some cases, such as in Chapter Two, were deliberately not chosen, or in other cases, had become secondary goals, in life situations that were affected too much by the daily struggles with illness.

Life phases and roles are associated with age and time norms. Characteristic of the long life with disability seems to be that it entails time patterns that are often different from what is considered to be normal and 'on time'. *Too early* was a salient theme. This encompassed having to leave working life too early, bodily deterioration and reduced functions occurring too early, but also the need to enter adult life too early as a strategy to meet expected and unavoidable impairments – these are illustrative examples. However, *too late* was also a salient theme: too late to start advanced studies due to deteriorating health, too late to get an independent life for the caregiving older parent in spite of the fact that the child had become an adult. Furthermore, too late for the mentally disabled to have a normal old age, after a long life afflicted by illness, and who sometimes lived in an institutionalised context. However, there was also a contrasting pattern: *it is never too late*, as expressed, with confidence, by the ageing disability movement activists in Chapter Four, and by the disabled couples in Chapter Seven. Some had established their couplehood rather late in life.

An important common theme in the life stories described in the chapters was that the long life with disability was associated with chronic conditions. Furthermore, repetitive illness complications and gradual bodily decline was a salient theme to various degrees. An important conclusion is that disabilities are seldom static. A long life with disability could usually not be understood as a 'consequence of passed illness', but as an existence where illness and illness complications continued to shape the lifecourse over the years. A long life with disability implies a particular *ageing* experience where the many years with disability give later life a particular signature. The chapters suggest that the phenomenon of ageing is intimately linked with various temporal dimensions. It was hard to distinguish the social effects of ageing from the impact of having lived a long life with disabilities and the personal experiences that stemmed from this. When the participants spoke of themselves, others and of social positions, a recurring theme was that age and ageing seemed to be of secondary importance to the experience of the long life with illness and impairment. These results are in agreement with what Zarb and Oliver (1993) found in their study of ageing with a disability. They remarked that the biographical stories they collected seemed to indicate that disabled people's experiences as older people were not nearly as important as 'their collective experience built around the prior experience of disability' (p 59). The long life with disability in many cases seems less shaped by age-graded life transitions than by illness changes that blur the boundaries between the phases of life. This is important knowledge.

Lives in a historical context

The historical period that forms the time frame for this book is the era from 1960 up to the present, in Sweden. What have we really found out about the imprints of this era on individuals' lives? There were important breakthroughs and successes in disability politics and reforms, but were these significant in the lives of the participants? There are no easy answers to this question. The impacts of different reforms and policies seem ambiguous. The participants in the different studies had varying opinions about the relative success of disability reforms depending on life situation and societal position, and the salience of the question to them. The question of reforms was very important to the interviewed activists of the Swedish disability movement described in Chapter Three. Although they pointed out significant successes, they also underlined that the path towards full participation was marked with difficulties. A common pattern was, however, that some reforms were not even mentioned, perhaps taken for granted by participants, while others were brought forward in most narratives as important breakthroughs, and in an almost set manner. The most prominent example was the legislation on assistance which seemed to be of both great ideological and practical significance. The right to assistance "changed our lives altogether", as one participant expressed it. This reform was associated with considerable *enabling* possibilities. For instance, it made it possible to live a very active 'third-age life', in spite of extensive disabilities. Yet over the years, some of the paradoxical shortcomings connected with the reforms in daily life had also become apparent: the difficulties of maintaining integrity and privacy and of having a 'back stage' in a daily life that was structured around the presence of personal assistants was a problem mentioned by many participants (for instance, in Chapters Six and Seven). They described strategies that they had developed to create a 'free zone' – privacy without assistants. The concepts of autonomy and independence thus take on many meanings. On the other hand, despite this reform, the study of parents with disabled children in Chapter Six showed that the parents still had a huge care responsibility for their adult disabled children, sometimes despite personal assistance 24 hours a day. Looking back on the life stories in the studies it becomes apparent that the reform of assistance has a limited reach in various ways – both intended and unintended ones.

Some of the participants incurred their severe disabilities as younger adults. For them, some disability reforms in the area of employment had been a precondition for being able to get a job or to continue work life at all. The verdict from the leaders in the disability movement was harsh: these reforms had been a failure and had opened very few job opportunities to disabled people. With the lifecourse approach it also became apparent how difficult it was to keep employment over time for those who had a job at the onset of their impairment, and how limited the impact of policies and reforms in the employment area actually were. Furthermore, 'the right to work' did not necessarily mean participation through a 'real work task'. This was a painful, recurring experience among the participants in the 30-year study described in Chapter Two. A related but somewhat different work pattern concerned being limited to employment in the 'disability field'. However, some groups were just too far away from the labour market or too ill to be considered for a job. This seemed particularly common among the mentally disabled people.

One set of reforms was hardly mentioned by some participants as having been important or having had an impact on life, yet in many ways it frames the era and constitutes a point of departure for the type of long lives with disability described in this volume. This was the de-institutionalisation process, which had far-reaching implications for disabled people and their families. The importance of this change was, however, pointed out by the activists in Chapter Three and by the parents in Chapter Six, from their different points of view. De-institutionalisation was actually intended to enable people to live modern lives with disability. As seen in Chapter Six, it represented a major shift in patterns of responsibility and caring roles for families where there was a disabled child. Yet it was a shift that had not always brought the anticipated positive consequences in the lives of disabled people, for instance, mentally disabled people, as seen in Chapter Five. A great gap between the visions and factual changes in living conditions had persisted, according to the mentally disabled participants and the caregiving parents.

The overshadowing illness and disability

During the first half of the era in focus in this volume, the medical model dominated in understanding impairment and disability more than it does today. In contrast to the medical model, the social model and the 'Nordic relational model of disability' focus on how society and environmental factors contribute to disability. Several of the chapters in this book bear witness to how important these models have been for improving disabled people's rights, chances of autonomy and participation. But, at the same time, is it possible that these social and relational models may have been too one-sided, with a tendency to underplay other important aspects of the experience of being disabled? An overall conclusion from our chapters is that neither of the models suffice when it comes to understanding or conceptualising the full meaning of living and ageing with disability. This becomes particularly apparent when the lifecourse approach is adopted. Experiences of a mental or physical illness or of the injured/ill body do not 'disappear' just by taking on a relational or social model, nor do they go away, despite adaptive measures to increase participation. The subjective, overshadowing experience of illness and body over the years, in spite of environmental and social adjustments, is a pattern with various expressions in the studies on which the chapters are based – all except for, perhaps, the study in Chapter Three, where the pioneers in the disability movement were interviewed. Here, disability as associated with stable person-environment arrangements and 'the absence of illness' seemed to have become 'the norm' in self-understanding within the disability movement. However, over time, few disabilities seem to have such stable properties. One important reason for this is that the majority of disabilities are caused by chronic illness. Even among very active people living successful third age lives, such as those described in Chapter Four, there were concerns that illness complications would destroy future possibilities for keeping that lifestyle. Rather than mirroring compensated person-environment solutions, the long life with disability often has the character of a series of ongoing transitional processes, due to continued illness complications and functional loss. The intrusive character of certain illnesses, for instance, of mental illness, makes them very difficult to compensate for at all. The many years with illness often seem to aggravate these conditions as well. Many illnesses change with age, but mostly the situation seems related to having the illness for a long period of time. To observe one's body and "feel it out" became a strategy for retaining control in everyday life for the participants in some of the studies. A corresponding pattern was seen among the mentally disabled participants where 'being one's illness', and somehow handling that situation, permeated everyday life.

It is easy to think that a person with multiple diagnoses and disabilities eventually "gets used to" living with disability and can better handle illness complications. An argument of that kind was in fact expressed by some of the activists in Chapter Three. However, there is not much evidence of this in the other chapters of this volume. Very few of the participants said that either old age or a long experience of disability made it easier to confront further health complications and additional functional limitations. It should be noted, however, that there were a few exceptions – Chapter Two described some ageing participants who had a feeling of increased confidence, after 30 years, about handling new complications. But being used to the illness does not make up for the losses. For several participants, described in Chapters Two, Five and Six, their life situation could be characterised as a series of crises that they had had to adapt to over the lifecourse. Bury (1982) coined the term 'biographical disruption' which has had a huge impact on trying to understand illness as a disruption in the ongoing lifecourse. The concept seems to suggest, however, a *single* big and unexpected event. An important conclusion is therefore that the concept does not fully capture the illness experience over the whole lifecourse where changes may be multiple and may be both unexpected *and* expected, as revealed by our results.

Old age after many years of disability

What does old age mean after a long life with disability? Is this stage characterised by 'double difference', or is life gradually 'normalised' with age in that one's life begins to look more like those of other older people? The answer, it seems, is both. Also in this regard, contrasting images emerged from the different chapters. In some ways, life seemed to become more like that of other people. In other ways, the unique experience of having lived a long life of disability *continued* to shape life in old age. The results indicate that for many of the participants, their impairments had worsened and increased over time. They experienced these aggravations as very limiting, in spite of the fact that they seemed to be 'freed' of other demands, like other retired people. As previously mentioned, disabilities often entail complications and additional impairments over the years. To still successfully manage one's situation – to retain the ability to go out and to participate in social activities, for example – came up as an important theme. Activities and choices made earlier in life also shaped the life of the pensioner. For instance, for those who had been active in disability organisations, later life was very much shaped by those many years invested working in the disability movement. Their life stories showed how this could be central to one's identity – including in later life. This group gained a positive disability identity, formed by their political life. A contrasting pattern was found, however, in Chapter Five, where the mentally disabled participants described identities that were negatively shaped by their mental illness.

A number of participants lived a life surprisingly similar to 'a regular modern pensioner's life', despite their special situation, as illustrated in Chapter Four. A conclusion that can be drawn is that some disabled seniors today have the possibility to live active, outgoing and self-fulfilling third age lives. To some degree this is also true for the disabled couples described in Chapter Seven. Many disabled pensioners described how they went to the theatre, were active in clubs or disability organisations or travelled abroad. However, Chapters Two and Five refuted the generality of this pattern: most of the participants had gradually lost – or never had – the chance of leading a third age lifestyle. In fact, the experience of growing old and becoming a pensioner as *a major life transition* was absent in these life stories: to be old did not imply anything 'new' or anything different. Life continued as usual. Furthermore, as demonstrated in Chapter Six, for the parents of disabled adult children the step to retirement had made it obvious how their lives *did not* conform to normative social roles. Their 'atypical' life as pensioners became more visible over time, especially in relation to norms about being a senior and generational care patterns.

These findings challenge in two ways dominant gerontological ideas and conceptualisations about successful ageing and the third age. On the one hand, the criteria for achieving successful ageing are not necessarily dependent on physical ability. Compensated in the right way, through environmental adjustments and personal assistance, and so on, it is possible to live outgoing and 'public' lives with extensive physical disabilities in old age. But on the other hand, it is clear that there are groups of people with severe disabilities that do not have the chance to live or have access to a third age life. The invasive character of the illness – physical or mental – has simply made such a later life impossible and out of reach. In these cases, as shown in Chapters Two and Five, old age has turned out to be limited and 'private', resembling more the criteria of being in the fourth age. It should be pointed out that these findings not only challenge key principles about successful ageing; They also challenge dominant norms about what a life with disability 'ought to be' in order to embody modern disability ideals and to be accomplished.

Time, disability and the multi-meanings of care

Another central theme discussed in the book is the multifaceted meaning of care in the context of disability and ageing. As demonstrated, in particular in Chapters Six and Seven, disabled people's situation of informal care has, until recently, hardly been explored, and the caregiver (as well as the care receiver) often seems non-existent, in policy as well as in research. The ambiguousness of the care concept in relation to disability has led to the invisibility of the carer, but also the invisibility of the meaning of the care. However, the chapters' detailed exploration of understanding care among ageing disabled couples and ageing parents reveals the significance of such help and care from and within the family. It is clearly shown that care permeates their lives, albeit in different ways. The life stories of the interviewed parents were characterised by a lifelong care responsibility, revealing a complex parental role that included balancing practical as well as emotional caring, and advocating for the adult child's rights. In the case of disabled couples, the mutual spousal care is part of making everyday life work, but is also important for helping them maintain closeness and integrity as a couple.

What is revealed from the participants' accounts in both studies, but from different perspectives, are themes describing care as an expression of interdependence and reciprocal relationships. In other words, care – as described and experienced by the participants – was not necessarily seen as opposed to the struggle for autonomy, participation and independence. The long time with care, and disability within close relationships, show that care is more than task-oriented, instrumental activities. Indeed, care encompasses several layers of meaning.

Several of the other chapters do not directly address the issue of care. However, it is possible to discern in some of the participants' stories that the role of family seemed to become increasingly important over time. It is also important to underline that we should not take for granted that disabled people always need help and care. Indeed, some of the participants in the chapters managed all by themselves, despite extensive impairments. An interpretation of this could be that the image of being an independent, autonomous disabled individual does not include the 'need of care', and especially not from family members. Nevertheless, living and ageing with disability is not automatically related to care.

Concerns about the future

The lifecourse concerns the present, the past, but also the future. The future, particularly worries about it, was a repeating theme with varying connotations in the studies on which the chapters are based. In spite of the implementation of comprehensive disability policies in Sweden, several participants expressed uncertainty and strong concerns about things such as the possibility of getting assistance in the future and their chances of being able to carry on any activities that were important to them. The illness and the body were central to these concerns, which included: the worry of losing what few abilities they had, the worry that new and difficult complications would arise, the worry that family caregivers might disappear and the worry of premature death. As a contrast, the worries about the future for some of the mentally disabled participants were connected with a feeling that nothing would ever change; The miserable life of today would just continue. From the interviews in the different studies it seemed clear that worries increased with the passage of the years, as this entailed a gradually failing body and often increasing fatigue due to physical or mental illness. Uncertainty about the future made one highly aware of the brevity of life. With the body as the midpoint and given that disabilities are changing and unpredictable, the uncertainty about the future did not only concern the disabled person, but also the family – as was the case with the caregiving older parents, presented in Chapter Six, and, in its particular way, the caregiving couples in Chapter Seven. They worried about their common future as well as that of their disabled partner. Ageing implies changes of many kinds. Functional decline and illness trajectories, combined with ageing, make the future particularly uncertain, and the strategies to handle this situation varied. A strategy expressed in many of the interviews was to live with 'double agendas' – that is, to think of the future both in the long and short term. But some of the participants, not least those who had mental illness, seemed to avoid thinking about the future altogether. Despite an awareness and acceptance that they might not live so long, the caregiving older parents continued to plan and prepare for the future. This meant that they were trying to create the best conditions for their ageing disabled children before they themselves became frail and died. An overall conclusion is that satisfaction over personal assistance and other social services was an important factor in how the future was met, but equally important was the proximity of informal help through family and close social contacts.

Conclusion

This book has adopted a particular lifecourse perspective on ageing. The intention was to illuminate multiple facets of ageing, disability and lifecourse in a modern society. The *intersection between age and disability* brings to the fore new and original insights concerning the meaning of growing old and being old, as well as about what it means to live and age with early onset disabilities. This intersection has, to date, been studied to a very limited extent and, in our opinion, this book adds new knowledge to a field of scholarship that needs to be further developed and where more research is needed.

Illustrative examples have been given throughout the book, disclosing that it can be hard to separate the experience of ageing from the experience of a *long life with disability*. Concepts such as *third age, fourth age* and *successful ageing* fail to fully capture that ageing and old age are far more complex and entail experiences that point to much more fluid boundaries between different life phases and age norms in later life than is usually acknowledged. There is a continuing need for research that empirically and theoretically challenges dominant theories on ageing and old age and which, in an unbiased way, explores the many-sided prerequisites and conditions of ageing.

At the same time, the lifecourse approach and the focus on time with disability that has been adopted in this book challenge the social model as the sole framework to understanding disability. Certain scholars have argued that, today, the lifecourse is increasingly de-institutionalised and characterised by fluid age norms and multiple identities (see, for instance, Hockey and James, 2003; Grenier, 2012). The lifecourse of disabled people may, in its own particular way, be an illustration of this point (also see Jeppsson Grassman, 2005). *The lifecourse approach* reveals important insights about the impact of multiple disabilities on life over time. There are important conclusions to be drawn for future research but also for practical work.

The book also highlights *the meaning of care* in previously unexplored contexts, such as where ageing parents are caregivers, or regarding mutual care in disabled couples. The results presented in this volume indicate, in various ways, how care is more than just task-oriented, instrumental activities. Here, the volume contributes to areas of knowledge which have, to date, been totally neglected, and where there is a need for continued research.

References

Bury, M. (1982) 'Chronic illness as biographical disruption', *Sociology of Health and Illness*, vol 4, no 2, pp 167–82.

Grenier, A. (2012) *Transitions and the lifecourse: Challenging the constructions of 'growing old'*, Bristol: The Policy Press.

Hockey, J. and James, A. (2003) *Growing up and growing old: Ageing and dependency in the life course*, London: Sage Publications.

Jeppsson Grassman, E. (2005) 'Tid, rum, kropp och livslopp. Nya perspektiv på funktionshinder' ['Time, space, body and life course. Disability from new perspectives'], in E. Jeppsson Grassman and L.-Ch. Hydén (eds) *Kropp, livslopp och åldrande. Några samhällsvetenskapliga perspektiv* [*Body, life course and ageing. Some social perspectives*], Lund: Studentlitteratur, pp 19-52.

Zarb, G. and Oliver, M. (1993) *Ageing with a disability: What do they expect after all these years?*, London: University of Greenwich.

Index

Page references for notes are followed by n

CPSIA information can be obtained
at www.ICGtesting.com
Printed in the USA
LVHW062031290821
696383LV00004B/467

9 781447 305224